William Beloe

Egypt and Scythia

Described by Herodotus, Book II and Part of Book IV

William Beloe

Egypt and Scythia
Described by Herodotus, Book II and Part of Book IV

ISBN/EAN: 9783337214258

Printed in Europe, USA, Canada, Australia, Japan

Cover: Foto ©ninafisch / pixelio.de

More available books at **www.hansebooks.com**

HE MEXICAN HAIR RENEWER.	FLORILINE *FOR THE TEETH.*
events the Hair Falling Out.	Is the Best Known Dentifrice.
stores Grey Hair to its Natural Colour.	Renders the Teeth Pearly White.
not a Dye.	Makes the Gums Hard and Healthy.
ntains no Colouring Matter.	Stops all Decay.
omotes Growth.	Gives a Fragrance to the Breath.
adicates Dandruff.	Removes Unpleasant Odours from the Mouth.
eps the Hair Perfectly Clean.	Removes the Smell of Tobacco Smoke.
es not Soil the Hands.	Is Delicious to the Taste,
Delicately Perfumed.	And is the Greatest Toilet Discovery of the Age.
old by Medicine Dealers l Perfumers everywhere. ice 3s. 6d. per bottle.	Sold by Chemists and Perfumers everywhere at 2s. 6d. per case.

OVENTRY MACHINISTS' Co.
(LIMITED.)

OLDEST AND LARGEST MAKERS OF

BICYCLES & TRICYCLES

IN THE WORLD.

| Catalogues Free by Post. |

Works: COVENTRY.

"IMPERIAL CLUB." LONDON: 15 & 16, Holborn Viaduct.

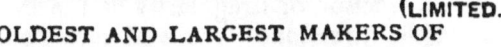

TO MOTHERS!
WOODWARD'S "GRIPE WATER,"

Or INFANTS' PRESERVATIVE. The only SAFE Medicine for all Disorders of Infants—Convulsions, Diarrhœa, Griping Pains, *Teething*, &c. A HIGH-CLASS MEDICINE, largely used by Doctors in their own families—the highest testimony to its value.

Sold by all Chemists and Stores, 1s. 1½d.
Sent post free for 14 Stamps by

WOODWARD, CHEMIST, NOTTINGHAM.

A WONDERFUL MEDICINE

BEECHAM'S PILLS

Are admitted by thousands to be worth above a Guinea a Box for Bilious and Nervous Disorders, such as Wind and Pain in the Stomach, Sick Headache, Giddiness, Fulness and Swelling after meals, Dizziness and Drowsiness, Cold Chills, Flushings of Heat, Loss of Appetite, Shortness of Breath, Costiveness, Scurvy, Blotches on the Skin, Disturbed Sleep, Frightful Dreams, and all Nervous and Trembling Sensations, &c. The first dose will give relief in 20 minutes. This is no fiction, for they have done it in thousands of cases. Every sufferer is earnestly invited to try one box of these Pills, and they will be acknowledged to be

WORTH A GUINEA A BOX.

For Females of all ages these Pills are invaluable, as a few doses of them carry off all humours, and bring about all that is required. No female should be without them. There is no medicine to be found to equal BEECHAM'S PILLS for removing any obstruction or irregularity of the system. If taken according to the directions given with each box, they will soon restore females of all ages to sound and robust health.

For a Weak Stomach, Impaired Digestion, and all Disorders of the Liver they act like "Magic," and a few doses will be found to work wonders upon the most important organs of the human machine. They strengthen the whole muscular system, restore the long-lost complexion, bring back the keen edge of appetite, and arouse into action, with the Rosebud of Health, the whole physical energy of the human frame. These are "facts" admitted by thousands, embracing all classes of society, and one of the best guarantees to the Nervous and Debilitated is BEECHAM'S PILLS have the largest sale of any patent medicine in the world.

Full Directions are given with each Box.
Sold by all Druggists and Patent Medicine Dealers in the United Kingdom, in Boxes at 1s. 1½d. and 2s. 9d. each. [30

INTRODUCTION.

HERODOTUS was born in the year 484 before Christ, at Halicarnassus. Halicarnassus was a Greek city founded upon rock, commanding a harbour on the coast of Asia Minor. It was on the north side of what is now a gulf, known, from the modern name of Halicarnassus, as the Gulf of Boudroun. The city had been founded by a colony of Dorians from Argolis. Herodotus belonged to a chief family in the town. His father was named Lyxes, and his mother Dryo. One of his uncles, Panyasis, was an epic poet. The birth date of Herodotus was six years after the battle of Marathon, and four years before the battles of Thermopylæ and Salamis. To tell the history of the war between the Greeks and Persians became the ambition of his life, and he went upon far travels in search of information.

When Herodotus was born, Artemisia, daughter of a Lygdamis, ruled over Halicarnassus, Cos, Nisyrus, and Calydna, in the interest of Xerxes, whom she joined as a volunteer with five ships at the battle of Salamis. A grandson of hers, another Lygdamis, became tyrant of Halicarnassus, and about the year B.C. 457 this Lygdamis put to death the poet uncle of Herodotus, Panyasis, who had written the exploits of Hercules in fourteen books and nine thousand verses. Herodotus, then about twenty-seven years old, left Halicarnassus and went to Samos, an island in the Ægean, about twenty-five miles long, where he stayed some time and acquired the dialect of the Ionians. Afterwards he returned to Halicarnassus and took part in freeing his native city from the tyranny of Lygdamis. But he departed again, and perhaps they were the next years of his life that he spent in travel and research. He visited all the chief places of Greece and Asia Minor, travelled in Thrace and Scythia, explored Egypt, went to Tyre, and through Phœnicia and Palestine, and made his way to Babylon.

But he set up his home at Thurium, a Greek colony in southern Italy, on the Gulf of Tarentum. It was founded after the ruin of the rich city of Sybaris by intestine feuds. Sybaris, whose luxury made the name of Sybarite proverbial, was destroyed by diversion of a river into it, and some of its fugitive citizens joined afterwards in the establishment of a new colony, of Athenian and other Greeks, near the site of the lost Sybaris, and from a spring there, called Thuria, they named their new home Thurium. This colony was first founded when **Herodotus** was about forty years old, and he was among the Greeks who settled there. He lived to be an old man, died at Thurium, and was there buried.

There is tradition of Herodotus at the Olympic Festival, reciting his History, moving the young Thucydides to tears of emotion, and having its nine books named after the nine Muses by the assembled Greeks in their enthusiasm. It is more likely that they were so named by some later grammarian, for the History contains passages that could only have been written when the historian was more than seventy years old, and it broke off unfinished, as if at the finish of the writer's life. It was the free and simple utterance of an old man who loved truth and the poets, took deep interest in life, on the Divine side as well as the human, and had seen many men and many lands, studying all with special reference to the History that he had planned for his life's work. As he wrote on, the fulness of his store, and thoroughness in telling what he had to tell, caused him to broaden out into explanatory episodes, of which the most famous is the account of Egypt given in his volume. When Egypt came, with the accession of Cambyses, into the history of Persian wars, Herodotus must needs tell what that Egypt was, for he liked to be thorough.

This account of Egypt, complete in itself, is an episode occupying the whole second book of the History, which is named, after the muse, "Euterpe." The shorter account of Scythia, here added to it, is given in like manner when Darius marches to attack the Scythians, and is an episode, complete in itself, that forms only a part of the fourth book, "Melpomene."

The Scythians of Herodotus occupied lands extending from the region of the Danubian Principalities to the Crimea. Their chief rivers were the Ister (now Danube), the Tyras (now Dniester), Hypanis (now Bog), Borysthenes (now Dnieper), and Tanaïs (now Don).   H. M.

Egypt Described by Herodotus.

1. CAMBYSES, the son of Cyrus, by Cassandana, daughter of Phanaspe, succeeded his father. The wife of Cyrus had died before him; he had lamented her loss himself with the sincerest grief, and commanded all his subjects to exhibit public marks of sorrow. Cambyses thus descended, considered the Ionians and Æolians as his slaves by right of inheritance. He undertook, therefore, an expedition against Egypt, and assembled an army for this purpose, composed as well of his other subjects, as of those Greeks who acknowledged his authority.

2. Before the reign of their king Psammetichus, the Egyptians esteemed themselves the most ancient of the human race; but when this prince came to the throne he took considerable pains to investigate the truth of this matter; the result was, that they believe the Phrygians more ancient than themselves, and themselves than the rest of mankind. Whilst Psammetichus was engaged in this inquiry, he contrived the following as the

most effectual means of removing his perplexity. He procured two children just born, of humble parentage, and gave them to a shepherd to be brought up among his flocks. He was ordered never to speak before them; to place them in a sequestered hut, and at proper intervals to bring them goats, whose milk they might suck whilst he was attending to other employments. His object was to know what word they would first pronounce articulately. The experiment succeeded to his wish; the shepherd complied with each particular of his directions, and at the end of two years, on his one day opening the door of their apartment, both the children extended their hands towards him, as if in supplication, and pronounced the word Becos. It did not at first excite his attention, but on their repeating the same expression whenever he appeared he related the circumstance to his master, and at his command, brought the children to his presence. When Psammetichus had heard them repeat this same word, he endeavoured to discover among what people it was in use: he found it was the Phrygian name for bread. From seriously revolving this incident, the Egyptians were induced to allow the Phrygians to be of greater antiquity than themselves.

3. That this really happened, I myself heard at Memphis from the priests of Vulcan. The Greeks,

among other idle tales, relate, that Psammetichus gave the children to be nursed by women whose tongues were previously cut out. During my residence at Memphis, the same priests informed me of many other curious particulars: but to be better satisfied how well the narrative which I have given on their authority was supported, I made it my business to visit Thebes and Heliopolis, the inhabitants of which latter place are deemed the most ingenious of all the Egyptians. I shall not think it expedient to say what I heard of their religious customs, more than the names of their deities, believing that all are well informed on this subject. Whatever I may say will be merely what my narrative requires.

4. In all which they related of human affairs, they were uniform and consistent with each other: they agree that the Egyptians first defined the measure of the year, which they divided into twelve parts; in this they affirm the stars to have been their guides. Their mode of computation is in my opinion more sagacious than that of the Greeks, who, for the sake of adjusting the seasons accurately, add every third year an intercalary month. The Egyptians divide their year into twelve months, giving to each month thirty days: by adding five days to every year, they have a uniform revolution of time. The people of this

country first invented the names of the twelve gods, and from them the Grecians borrowed them. They were the first also who erected altars, shrines, and temples; and none before them ever engraved the figures of animals on stone; the truth of all which they sufficiently authenticate. The name of their first king was Menes, in whose reign the whole of Egypt, except the province of Thebes, was one extended marsh. No part of all that district, which is now situate beyond the lake Mœris, was then to be seen, the distance between which lake and the sea is a journey of seven days.

5. The account which they give of their country appears just and reasonable. It must be obvious to the inspection of any one of common sagacity, even though he knew it not before, that the part of Egypt to which the Greeks now sail formerly constituted a part of the bed of the river; this may constantly be observed of all that tract of country beyond the lake, to pass over which would employ a journey of three days; but this the Egyptians themselves do not assert. Of this fact there exists another proof: if from a vessel bound to Egypt, the lead be thrown at the distance of a day's sailing from the shore, it will come up at the depth of eleven fathoms covered with mud, plainly indicating that it was brought there by the water.

6. According to our limitation of Egypt, which

is from the bay of Plinthene to lake Serbonis, near mount Casius, the whole extent of the coast is sixty schæni. It may not be improper to remark, that they who have smaller portions of land, measure them by orgyæ, they who have larger by stadia, such as have considerable tracts by parasangs. The schœnus, which is an Egyptian measure, used in the mensuration of more extensive domains, is equivalent to sixty stadia, as the parasang is to thirty. Agreeably to such mode of computation, the coast of Egypt towards the sea is in length three thousand six hundred stadia.

7. From hence inland to Heliopolis, the country of Egypt is a spacious plain, which, though without water, and on a declivity, is a rich and slimy soil. The distance betwixt Heliopolis and the sea is nearly the same as from the altar of the twelve deities, at Athens, to the shrine of Jupiter Olympus, at Pisa. Whoever will be at the trouble to ascertain this point, will not find the difference to exceed fifteen stadia: the distance from Pisa to Athens wants precisely fifteen stadia of one thousand five hundred, which is the exact number of stadia betwixt Heliopolis and the sea.

8. From Heliopolis to the higher parts of Egypt, the country becomes more narrow, and is confined on one part by a long chain of Arabian mountains, which, from the north, stretch south and south-

west, in a regular inclination to the Red Sea. The pyramids of Memphis were built with stones drawn from these mountains, which from hence have a winding direction towards the places we have before described. I have been informed, that to travel along this range of hills, from east to west, which is the extreme length of the country, will employ a space of two months: they add, that the eastern parts abound in aromatics. On that side of Egypt which lies towards Libya, there is another steep and sandy mountain, on which certain pyramids have been erected: these extend themselves, like those Arabian hills which stretch towards the south. Thus the country beyond Heliopolis differs exceedingly from the rest of Egypt, and may be passed in a journey of four days. The intermediate space betwixt these mountains is an open plain, in its narrowest part not more in extent than two hundred stadia, measuring from the Arabian to what is called the Libyan mountain, from whence Egypt becomes again wider.

9. From Heliopolis to Thebes is a voyage of about nine days, or a space of four thousand eight hundred and sixty stadia, equivalent to eighty-one schœni. I have before observed, that the length of the Egyptian coast is three thousand six hundred stadia; from the coast to Thebes is six thousand

one hundred and twenty stadia; from Thebes to Elephantine eight hundred and twenty.

10. The greater part of the country described above, as I was informed by the priests (and my own observation induced me to be of the same opinion) has been a gradual acquisition to the inhabitants. The country above Memphis, between the hills before mentioned, seems formerly to have been an arm of the sea, and is not unlike the region about Ilium, Teuthrania, Ephesus, and the plain of the Meander, if we may be allowed to compare small things with great. It must certainly be allowed, that none of the streams which water the above country may in depth or in magnitude compare with any one of the five arms of the Nile. I could mention other rivers, which, though inferior to the Nile, have produced many wonderful effects; of these, the river Achelous is by no means the least considerable. This flows through Acarnania, and, losing itself in the sea which washes the Echinades, has connected one half of those islands with the continent.

11. In Arabia, at no great distance from Egypt, there is a long but narrow bay, diverging from the Erythrean Sea, which I shall more minutely describe. Its extreme length, from the straits where it commences, to where it communicates with the main, will employ a bark with oars a voyage of forty

days, but its breadth in the widest parts may be sailed over in half a day. In this bay, the tide daily ebbs and flows; and I conceive that Egypt itself was a gulf formerly of similar appearance, and that, issuing from the Northern Ocean, it extended itself towards Ethiopia; in the same manner the Arabian one so described, rising in the south, flowed towards Syria; and that the two were only separated from each other by a small neck of land. If the Nile should by any means have an issue into the Arabian gulf, in the course of twenty thousand years it might be totally choked up with earth brought there by the passage of the river. I am of opinion that this might take place even within ten thousand years: why then might not a gulf still greater than this be choked up with mud in the space of time which has passed before our age, by a stream so great and powerful as the Nile?

12. All, therefore, that I heard from the natives concerning Egypt, was confirmed by my own observations. I remarked also, that this country gains upon the region which it joins; that shells are found upon the mountains; and that an acrid matter exudes from the soil, which has proved injurious even to the pyramids; and that the only mountain in Egypt which produces sand is the one situate above Memphis. Neither does Egypt

possess the smallest resemblance to Arabia, on which it borders, nor to Libya and Syria, for the sea-coast of Arabia is possessed by Syrians. It has a black and crumbling soil, composed of such substances as the river in its course brings down from Ethiopia. The soil of Libya we know to be red and sandy; and the earth, both of Arabia and Syria, is strong and mixed with clay.

13. The information of the priests confirmed the account which I have already given of this country. In the reign of Mœris, as soon as the river rose to eight cubits, all the lands above Memphis were overflowed; since which a period of about nine hundred years has elapsed; but at present, unless the river rises to sixteen, or at least fifteen cubits, its waters do not reach those lands.

If the ground should continue to elevate itself as it has hitherto done, by the river's receding from it, the Egyptians below the lake Mœris, and those who inhabit the Delta, will be reduced to the same perplexity which they themselves affirm menaces the Greeks. For as they understand that Greece is fertilised and refreshed by rain, and not by rivers like their own, they predict that the inhabitants, trusting to their usual supplies, will probably suffer the miseries of famine; meaning, that as they have no resource, and only such water as the clouds supply, they must inevitably perish if disappointed of rain at the proper seasons.

14. Such being the just sentiments of the Egyptians with respect to Greece, let us inquire how they themselves are circumstanced. If, as I before remarked, the country below Memphis, which is that where the water has receded, should progressively, from the same cause, continue to extend itself, the Egyptians who inhabit it might have still juster apprehensions of suffering from famine. For in that case, their lands, which are never fertilised by rain, could not receive benefit from the overflowings of the river. The people who possess that district, of all mankind, and even of all the Egyptians, enjoy the fruits of the earth with the smallest labour. They have no occasion for the process nor the instruments of agriculture, which are usual and necessary in other countries. As soon as the river has spread itself over their lands, and returned to its bed, each man scatters the seed over his ground, and waits patiently for the harvest, without any other care than that of turning some swine into the fields, to tread down the grain. These are at the proper season again let loose, to shake the corn from the ear, which is then gathered.

15. If we follow the tradition of the Ionians, it will appear that all which may be properly

denominated Egypt is limited to the Delta. This region, from the watch-tower erected by Perseus, extends along the coast to the salt-pits of Pelusium, to the length of forty schæni. From the coast inland it stretches to the city of Cercasora, where the Nile divides itself into two branches, one of which is termed Pelusium, the other Canopus. Of the rest of Egypt, they affirm that part of it belongs to Libya, and part to Arabia, which, if it be true, we shall be obliged to conclude that formerly the Egyptians had no country at all. The Delta, as they themselves assert, and as I myself was convinced by observation, is still liable to be overflowed, and was formerly covered with water. Under these circumstances, their curiosity to examine whether they were the most ancient of the human race must seem preposterous, and their experiment of the two children to discover what language they should first speak, was absurd and unnecessary. For my own part, I am of opinion that the Egyptians did not commence their origin with the Delta, but from the first existence of the human race. That as their country became more extensive, some remained in their primitive places of residence, whilst others migrated to a lower situation. Hence it was that Thebes, comprising a tract of land which is six thousand one hundred and twenty stadia in circumference, went formerly under the name of Egypt.

16. If my opinion concerning Egypt be true, that of the Ionians must certainly be wrong; if, on the contrary, the Ionians are right in their conjecture, it will not be difficult to prove that the Greeks, as well as the Ionians, are mistaken in their account of the earth; of which they affirm that Europe, Asia, and Libya constitute the proper division: but if the Delta belong neither to Asia nor Libya, it makes by itself necessarily a fourth and distinct portion of the globe; for, according to the above mode of reasoning, the Nile cannot completely form the division between Asia and Libya; at the extremity of the Delta it is separated into two branches, and the country lying between cannot properly belong either to Asia or Libya.

17. Avoiding further comment upon the sentiments of the Ionians, I myself am of opinion that all the tract of country inhabited by Egyptians is properly termed Egypt, as the countries inhabited by the Cilicians and Assyrians are respectively denominated Cilicia and Assyria. I must also think that the land of Egypt alone constitutes the natural and proper limits of Asia and Libya. If we follow the opinion received among the Greeks, we are to consider the whole of Egypt commencing from the cataracts and the city Elephantine, as

divided into two parts, with distinct appellations, the one belonging to Libya, the other to Asia; the Nile, beginning at the cataract, flows through the centre of Egypt, and empties itself into the sea. As far as the city of Cercasora, it proceeds in one undivided channel, but it there separates itself into three branches: that which directs itself towards the east is called the Pelusian mouth, the Canopic inclines to the west; the third in one continued line meets the point of the Delta, which dividing in two, it finally pours itself into the sea; this arm is equally celebrated, and not inferior in the depth of its waters; it is called the Sebbennitic mouth, and this again divides itself into two branches; one is called the Saitic, and one the Mendesian channel; both empty themselves into the sea. There are two other mouths, the Bolbitinian and the Bucolic; these are not produced by nature, but by art.

18. My opinion concerning the extent of Egypt receives farther confirmation from the oracle of Ammon, of which, however, I had no knowledge till my mind was already satisfied on the subject. The people of Marea and Apis, who inhabit the borders of Libya, thinking themselves to be not Egyptians but Libyans, both of them disliked the religious ceremonies of the country, and that particular restriction which did not permit them to kill

heifers for food: they sent therefore to Ammon, declaring that they had no connection with the Egyptians; for they lived beyond the Delta, had their opinions and prejudices as distinct as possible, and wished to have no restriction in the article of food. The deity signified his disapprobation of their conduct, and intimated that every part of that region which was watered by the Nile was strictly to be denominated Egypt; and that all who dwelt below Elephantine, and drank of this stream, were Egyptians.

19. In its more extensive inundations, the Nile does not overflow the Delta only, but part of that territory which is called Libyan, and sometimes the Arabian frontier, and extends about the space of two days' journey on each side, speaking on an average. Of the nature of this river I could obtain no certain information from the priests or from others. It was, nevertheless, my particular desire to know why the Nile, beginning at the summer solstice, continues gradually to rise for the space of one hundred days, after which for the same space it as gradually recedes, remaining throughout the winter, and till the return of the summer solstice, in its former low and quiescent state: but all my inquiries of the inhabitants proved ineffectual, and I was unable to learn why the Nile was thus distinguished in its properties from other streams. I

was equally unsuccessful in my wishes to be informed why this river alone wafted no breeze from its surface.

20. From a desire of gaining a reputation for sagacity, this subject has employed the attention of many among the Greeks. There have been three different modes of explaining it, two of which merit no further attention than barely to be mentioned; one of them affirms the increase of the Nile to be owing to the Etesian winds, which by blowing in an opposite direction, impede the river's entrance to the sea. But it has often happened that no winds have blown from this quarter, and the phenomenon of the Nile has still been the same. It may also be remarked, that were this the real cause, the same events would happen to other rivers, whose currents are opposed to the Etesian winds, which, indeed, as having a less body of waters, and a weaker current, would be capable of still less resistance: but there are many streams, both in Syria and Libya, none of which exhibit the same appearances with the Nile.

21. The second opinion is still less agreeable to reason, though more calculated to excite wonder. This affirms, that the Nile has these qualities, as flowing from the ocean, which entirely surrounds the earth.

22. The third opinion, though more plausible in

appearance, is still more false in reality. It simply intimates that the body of the Nile is formed from the dissolution of snow, which coming from Libya through the regions of Ethiopia, discharges itself upon Egypt. But how can this river, descending from a very warm to a much colder climate, be possibly composed of melted snow? There are many other reasons concurring to satisfy any person of good understanding that this opinion is contrary to fact. The first and the strongest argument may be drawn from the winds, which are in these regions invariably hot: it may also be observed that rain and ice are here entirely unknown. Now if in five days after a fall of snow it must necessarily rain, which is indisputably the case, it follows, that if there were snow in those countries, there would certainly be rain. The third proof is taken from the colour of the natives, who from excessive heat are universally black; moreover the kites and the swallows are never known to migrate from this country: the cranes also, flying from the severity of a Scythian winter, pass that cold season here. If, therefore, it snowed although but little in those places through which the Nile passes, or in those where it takes its rise, reason demonstrates that none of the above-mentioned circumstances could possibly happen.

23. The argument which attributes to the ocean

these phenomena of the Nile seems rather to partake of fable than of truth or sense. For my own part, I know no river of the name of Oceanus; and am inclined to believe that Homer, or some other poet of former times, first invented and afterwards introduced it in his compositions.

24. But as I have mentioned the preceding opinions only to censure and confute them, I may be expected perhaps to give my own sentiments on this subject. It is my opinion that the Nile overflows in the summer season, because in the winter the sun, driven by the storms from his usual course, ascends into the higher regions of the air above Libya. My reason may be explained without difficulty; for it may be easily supposed, that to whatever region this power more nearly approaches, the rivers and streams of that country will be proportionably dried up and diminished.

25. If I were to go more at length into the argument, I should say that the whole is occasioned by the sun's passage through the higher parts of Libya. For as the air is invariably serene, and the heat always tempered by cooling breezes, the sun acts there as it does in the summer season, when his place is in the centre of the heavens. The solar rays absorb the aqueous particles, which their influence forcibly elevates into the higher

regions; here they are received, separated, and dispersed by the winds. And it may be observed, that the south and south-west, which are the most common winds in this quarter, are of all others most frequently attended with rain: it does not, however, appear to me, that the sun remits all the water which he every year absorbs from the Nile; some is probably withheld. As winter disappears he returns to the middle place of the heavens, and again by evaporation draws to him the waters of the rivers, all of which are then found considerably increased by the rains, and rising to their extreme heights. But in summer, from the want of rain, and from the attractive power of the sun, they are again reduced: but the Nile is differently circumstanced, it never has the benefit of rains, whilst it is constantly acted upon by the sun; a sufficient reason why it should in the winter season be proportionably lower than in summer. In winter the Nile alone is diminished by the influence of the sun, which in summer attracts the water of the rivers indiscriminately; I impute therefore to the sun the remarkable properties of the Nile.

26. To the same cause is to be ascribed, as I suppose, the state of the air in that country, which from the effect of the sun is always extremely rarefied, so that in the higher parts of Libya there

prevails an eternal summer. If it were possible to produce a change in the seasons, and to place the regions of the north in those of the south, and those of the south in the north, the sun, driven from his place by the storms of the north would doubtless affect the higher parts of Europe, as it now does those of Libya. It would also, I imagine, then act upon the waters of the Ister, as it now does on those of the Nile.

27. That no breeze blows from the surface of the river, may, I think, be thus accounted for:—Where the air is in a very warm and rarefied state, wind can hardly be expected, this generally rising in places which are cold. Upon this subject I shall attempt no further illustration, but leave it in the state in which it has so long remained.

28. In all my intercourse with Egyptians, Libyans, and Greeks, I have only met with one person who pretended to have any knowledge of the sources of the Nile. This was the priest who had the care of the sacred treasures in the temple of Minerva at Sais. He assured me, that on this subject he possessed the most unquestionable intelligence, though his assertions never obtained my serious confidence. He informed me, that betwixt Syene, a city of the Thebais, and Elephantine, there were two mountains, respectively terminating in an acute summit; the name of the

one was Crophi, of the other Mophi. He affirmed, that the sources of the Nile, which were fountains of unfathomable depth, flowed from the centres of these mountains; that one of these streams divided Egypt, and directed its course to the north; the other, in like manner, flowed towards the south, through Ethiopia. To confirm his assertion, that those springs were unfathomable, he told me that Psammetichus, sovereign of the country, had ascertained it by experiment; he let down a rope of the length of several thousand orgyiæ, but could find no bottom. This was the priest's information, on the truth of which I presume not to determine. If such an experiment was really made, there might perhaps in these springs be certain vortices, occasioned by the reverberation of the water from the mountains, of force sufficient to buoy up the sounding line, and prevent its reaching the bottom.

29. I was not able to procure any other intelligence than the above, though I so far carried my inquiry, that, with a view of making observation, I proceeded myself to Elephantine: of the parts which lie beyond that city I can only speak from the information of others. Beyond Elephantine this country becomes rugged; in advancing up the stream it will be necessary to hale the vessel on each side by a rope, such as is used for oxen. If

this should give way, the impetuosity of the stream forces the vessel violently back again. To this place from Elephantine is a four days' voyage; and here, like the Meander, the Nile becomes winding, and for the space of twelve schæni there is no mode of proceeding but that above mentioned. Afterwards you come to a wide and spacious plain, and meet an island which stands in the centre of the river, and is called Tachompso. The higher part beyond Elephantine is possessed by the Ethiopians, who also inhabit half of this island, the other half belongs to Egyptians. In the vicinity of the island is an extensive lake, near which some Ethiopian shepherds reside; passing over this, you again enter into a channel of the Nile, which flows into the above lake. Beyond this it is necessary, for the space of about forty days, to travel on the banks of the river, which is here so impeded with rocks, as to render the passage in a vessel impossible. At the end of these forty days the traveller enters a second vessel, and after a voyage of twelve days will arrive at Meroe, a very considerable town, and as some say the capital of the rest of Ethiopia. The inhabitants pay divine honours to Jupiter and Bacchus only, but these they worship with the extremest veneration. At this place is an oracle of Jupiter, whose declarations they permit, with the most implicit obedience, to regulate all their martial expeditions.

30. Leaving this city at about the same distance as from hence to Elephantine, your bark will arrive at the country of the Automoli, who are also known by the name of Asmach. This word, translated into our language, signifies those who stand on the left hand of the sovereign. This people, to the amount of two hundred and forty thousand individuals, were formerly Egyptian warriors, and migrated to these parts of Ethiopia on the following occasion. In the reign of Psammetichus they were by his command stationed in different places; some were appointed for the defence of Elephantine against the Ethiopians, some at the Pelusian Daphne, others were detached to prevent the incursions of the Arabians and Assyrians; and to awe Libya there was a garrison also at Marea; at this present period the military stations are regulated by the Persians, as they were under king Psammetichus; for there are Persian garrisons now stationed at Elephantine and Daphne. When these Egyptians had remained for the space of three years in the above situation, without being relieved, they determined by general consent to revolt from Psammetichus to the Ethiopians; on intelligence of which event they were immediately followed by Psammetichus, who,

on his coming up with them, solemnly adjured them not to desert the gods of their country, their wives and their children. One of them is said to have behaved himself with rudeness, and to have replied, that they should doubtless have no difficulty in obtaining both wives and children. On their arrival in Ethiopia, the Automoli devoted themselves to the service of the monarch, who, in recompense for their conduct, assigned them a certain district of Ethiopia, possessed by a people in rebellion against him, whom he ordered them to expel for that purpose. After the establishment of the Egyptians among them, the tincture which they imbibed of Egyptian manners, had a very sensible effect in civilising the Ethiopians.

31. Thus, without computing that part of it which flows through Egypt, the course of the Nile is known to the extent of four months' journey, partly by land and partly by water; for it will be found on experience that no one can go in a less time from Elephantine to the Automoli. It is certain that the Nile rises in the west, but beyond the Automoli all is uncertainty, this part of the country being, from the excessive heat, a rude and uncultivated desert.

32. It may not be improper to relate an account which I received from certain Cyrenæans: On an

expedition which they made to the oracle of
Ammon, they said they had an opportunity of conversing with Etearchus, the sovereign of the
country: among other topics the Nile was mentioned, and it was observed, that the particulars of
its source were hitherto entirely unknown. Etearchus informed them, that some Nassamonians once
visited his court; (these are a people of Africa who
inhabit the Syrtes, and a tract of land which from
thence extends towards the east;) on his making
inquiry of them concerning the deserts of Libya,
they related the following incident: Some young
men, who were sons of persons of distinction, had
on their coming to man's estate signalised themselves by some extravagance of conduct. Among
other things, they deputed by lot five of their companions to explore the solitudes of Libya, and to
endeavour at extending their discoveries beyond all
preceding adventurers. All that part of Libya
towards the northern ocean from Egypt to the
promontory of Soloeis, which terminates the third
division of the earth, is inhabited by the different
nations of the Libyans, that district alone excepted in possession of the Greeks and Phœnicians. The remoter parts of Libya beyond the
sea-coast, and the people who inhabit its borders,
are infested by various beasts of prey; the country
yet more distant is a parched and immeasurable

desert. The young men left their companions, being well provided with water and with food, and first proceeded through the region which was inhabited; they next came to that which was infested by wild beasts, leaving which they directed their course westward through the desert. After a journey of many days, over a barren and sandy soil, they at length discerned some trees growing in a plain; these they approached, and seeing fruit upon them, they gathered it. Whilst they were thus employed, some men of dwarfish stature came where they were, seized their persons, and carried them away. They were mutually ignorant of each other's language, but the Nassamonians were conducted over many marshy grounds to a city, in which all the inhabitants were of the same diminutive appearance, and of a black colour. This city was washed by a great river, which flowed from west to east, and abounded in crocodiles.

33. Such was the conversation of Etearchus, as it was related to me; he added, as the Cyrenæans farther told me, that the Nassamonians returned to their own country, and reported the men whom they had met to be all of them magicians. The river which washed their city, according to the conjecture of Etearchus, which probability confirms, was the Nile. The Nile certainly rises in Libya, which it divides; and if it be allowable to draw conclu-

sions from things which are well known concerning those which are uncertain and obscure, it takes a similar course with the Ister. This river, commencing at the city of Pyrene, among the Celtæ, flows through the centre of Europe. These Celtæ are found beyond the columns of Hercules; they border on the Cynesians, the most remote of all the nations who inhabit the western parts of Europe. At that point which is possessed by the Istrians, a Milesian colony, the Ister empties itself into the Euxine.

34. The sources of the Ister, as it passes through countries well inhabited, are 'sufficiently notorious; but of the fountains of the Nile, washing as it does the rude and uninhabitable deserts of Libya, no one can speak with precision. All the knowledge which I have been able to procure from the most diligent and extensive inquiries, I have before communicated. Through Egypt it directs its course towards the sea. Opposite to Egypt are the mountains of Silicia, from whence to Sinope, on the Euxine, a good traveller may pass in five days: on the side immediately opposite to Sinope, the Ister is poured into the sea. Thus the Nile, as it traverses Libya, may properly enough be compared to the Ister. But on this subject I have said all that I think necessary.

35. Concerning Egypt itself I shall speak more at large; it claims our admiration beyond all other

countries, and the wonderful things which it exhibits demand a very copious description. The Egyptians, born under a climate to which no other can be compared, possessing a river different in its nature and properties from all the rivers in the world, are themselves distinguished from the rest of mankind by the singularity of their institutions and their manners. In this country the women leave to the men the management of the loom in the retirement of the house, whilst they themselves are engaged abroad in the business of commerce. Other nations in weaving shoot the woof above, the Egyptians beneath: here the men carry burdens on their heads, women on their shoulders; women stand erect and the men stoop when elsewhere the reverse is usual. The offices of nature are performed at home, but they eat their meals publicly in the streets. In vindication of this they assert that those things which, though necessary, are unseemly, are best done in private; but whatever has no shame attached to it should be done openly. The office of the priesthood is in every instance confined to the men; there are no priestesses in Egypt, in the service either of male or female deities; the men are under no obligation to support their parents, if unwilling to do so, but the women are.

36. The priests of the gods, who in other places wear their hair long, in Egypt wear it short. It is

elsewhere customary, in cases of death, for those who are most nearly related, to cut off their hair in testimony of sorrow; but the Egyptians, who at other times have their heads closely shorn, suffer the hair on this occasion to grow. Other nations will not suffer animals to approach the place of their repast; but in Egypt they live promiscuously with the people. Wheat and barley are common articles of food in other countries; but in Egypt they are thought mean and disgraceful; the diet here consists principally of spelt, a kind of corn which some call zea. Their dough they knead with their feet; whilst in the removal of mud and dung they do not scruple to use their hands. Male children, except in those places which have borrowed the custom from hence, are left in other nations as nature formed them; in Egypt they are circumcised. The men have two vests, the women only one. In opposition to the customs of other nations, the Egyptians fix the ropes to their sails on the inside. The Greeks, when they write or reckon with counters, go from the left to the right, the Egyptians from right to left; notwithstanding which they persist in affirming that the Greeks write to the left, but they themselves always to the right. They have two sorts of letters, one of which is appropriated to sacred subjects, the other used on common occasions.

37. Their veneration of their deities is superstitious to an extreme; one of their customs is to drink out of brazen goblets, which it is the universal practice among them to cleanse every day. They are so regardful of neatness that they wear only linen, and that always newly washed; and it is from the idea of cleanliness, which they regard much beyond comeliness, that they use circumcision. Their priests every third day shave every part of their bodies, to prevent vermin or any species of impurity from adhering to those who are engaged in the service of the gods. The priesthood is also confined to one particular mode of dress; they have one vest of linen, and their shoes are made of the byblus; they wash themselves in cold water twice in the course of the day, and as often in the night. It would indeed be difficult to enumerate their religious ceremonies, all of which they practise with superstitious exactness. The sacred ministers possess in return many and great advantages: they are not obliged to consume any part of their domestic property; each has a portion of the sacred viands, ready dressed, assigned him, besides a large and daily allowance of beef and of geese; they have also wine, but are not permitted to feed on fish.

Beans are sown in no part of Egypt, neither will the inhabitants eat them, either boiled or raw; the priests will not even look at this pulse, esteeming it exceedingly unclean. Every god has several attendant priests, and one of superior dignity, who presides over the rest; when any one dies, he is succeeded by his son.

38. They esteem bulls as sacred to Epaphus, which, previously to sacrifice, are thus carefully examined: if they can but discover a single black hair in his body, he is deemed impure; for this purpose a priest is particularly appointed, who examines the animal as it stands, and as reclined on its back; its tongue is also drawn out, and he observes whether it be free from those blemishes which are specified in their sacred books, and of which I shall speak hereafter. The tail also undergoes examination, every hair of which must grow in its natural and proper form. If in all these instances the bull appears to be unblemished, the priest fastens the byblus round his horns; he then applies a preparation of earth, which receives the impression of his seal, and the animal is led away; this seal is of so great importance, that to sacrifice a beast which has it not is deemed a capital offence.

39. I proceed to describe their mode of sacrifice:—Having led the animal destined and marked for the purpose to the altar, they kindle a fire; a libation of wine is poured upon the altar; the god

is solemnly invoked, and the victim then is killed; they afterwards cut off his head, and take the skin from the carcase; upon the head they heap many imprecations; such as have a market-place at hand carry it there, and sell it to the Grecian traders; if they have not this opportunity, they throw it into the river. They devote the head, by wishing that whatever evil menaces those who sacrifice, or Egypt in general, it may fall upon that head. This ceremony respecting the head of the animal, and this mode of pouring a libation of wine upon the altar, is indiscriminately observed by all the Egyptians; in consequence of the above, no Egyptian will on any account eat of the head of a beast. As to the examination of the victims, and their ceremony of burning them, they have different methods, as their different occasions of sacrifice require.

40. Of that goddess whom they esteem the first of all their deities, and in whose honour their greatest festival is celebrated, I shall now make more particular mention. After the previous ceremony of prayers, they sacrifice an ox; they then strip off the skin, and take out the intestines, leaving the fat and the paunch; they afterwards cut off the legs, the shoulders, the neck, and the extremities of the loin; the rest of the body is stuffed with fine bread, honey, raisins, figs, frank-

incense, and various aromatics; after this process they burn it, pouring upon the flame a large quantity of oil; whilst the victim is burning, the spectators flagellate themselves, having fasted before the ceremony; the whole is completed by their feasting on the residue of the sacrifice.

41. All the Egyptians sacrifice bulls without blemish, and calves; the females are sacred to Isis, and may not be used for this purpose. This divinity is represented under the form of a woman, and as the Greeks paint Io, with horns upon her head; for this reason the Egyptians venerate cows far beyond all other cattle, neither will any man or woman among them kiss a Grecian, nor use a knife, or spit, or any domestic utensil belonging to a Greek, nor will they eat even the flesh of such beasts as by their law are pure, if it has been cut with a Grecian knife. If any of these cattle die, they thus dispose of their carcases: the females are thrown into the river, the males they bury in the vicinity of the city, and, by way of mark, one and sometimes both of the horns are left projecting from the ground; they remain thus a stated time, and till they begin to putrefy, when a vessel appointed for this particular purpose is despatched from Prosopitis, an island of the Delta, nine schœni in extent, and containing several cities. Atar-

bechis, one of these cities, in which is a temple of Venus, provides the vessels for this purpose, which are sent to the different parts of Egypt. These collect and transport the bones of the animals, which are all buried in one appointed place. This law and custom extends to whatever cattle may happen to die, as the Egyptians themselves put none to death.

42. Those who worship in the temple of the Theban Jupiter, or belong to the district of Thebes, abstain from sheep, and sacrifice goats. The same deities receive in Egypt different forms of worship; the ceremonies of Isis and of Osiris, who they say is no other than the Grecian Bacchus, are alone unvaried; in the temple of Mendes, and in the whole Mendesian district, goats are preserved, and sheep sacrificed. Why the Thebans, and all who are under their influence, abstain from sheep is thus explained:—Jupiter, they say, was long averse to the earnest solicitations of Hercules to see his person; but in consequence of his repeated importunity, the god, in compliance, used the following artifice: He cut off the head of a ram, and, covering himself with its skin, showed himself in that form to Hercules. From this incident the Egyptian statues of Jupiter represent that divinity with the head of a ram. This custom was borrowed of the Egyptians by the Ammonians, who are com-

posed partly of Egyptians and partly of Ethiopians, and whose dialect is formed promiscuously of both those languages. The Egyptians call Jupiter Ammoun, and I should think this was the reason why the above people named themselves Ammonians. From this, however, it is that the Thebans esteem the ram as sacred, and, except on the annual festival of Jupiter, never put one to death. Upon this solemnity they kill a ram, and, placing its skin on the image of the god, they introduce before it a figure of Hercules; the assembly afterwards beat the ram, and conclude the ceremony by enclosing the body in a sacred chest.

43. This Hercules, as I have been informed, is one of the twelve great gods; but of the Grecian Hercules. I could in no part of Egypt procure any knowledge; that this name was never borrowed by Egypt from Greece, but certainly communicated by the Egyptians to the Greeks, and to those in particular who assign it to the son of Amphitryon, is among other arguments sufficiently evident from this, that both the reputed parents of this Hercules, Amphitryon and Alcmena, were of Egyptian origin. The Egyptians also disclaim all knowledge both of Neptune and the Dioscuri, neither of whom are admitted among the number of their gods. If they had ever borrowed the name of a deity from

Greece, the remembrance of these, so far from being less, must have been stronger than of any other; for if they then made voyages, and if, as I have great reason to believe, there were at that time Greek sailors, they would rather have been acquainted with the names of the other deities than with that of Hercules. Hercules is certainly one of the most ancient deities of Egypt; and, as they themselves affirm, is one of the twelve who were produced from the eight gods seventeen thousand years before the reign of Amasis.

44. From my great desire to obtain information on this subject, I made a voyage to Tyre, in Phœnicia, where is a temple of Hercules held in great veneration. Among the various offerings which enriched and adorned it, I saw two pillars; the one was of the purest gold, the other of emerald, which in the night diffused an extraordinary splendour. I inquired of the priests how long this temple had been erected, but I found that they also differed in their relation from the Greeks. This temple, as they affirmed, had been standing ever since the first building of the city, a period of two thousand three hundred years. I saw also at Tyre another temple consecrated to the Thasian Hercules. At Thasus, which I visited, I found a temple erected to this deity by the Phœnicians,

who built Thasus while they were engaged in search of Europa, an event which happened five generations before Hercules, the son of Amphitryon, was known in Greece. From all these circumstances I was convinced that Hercules must be a very ancient deity. Such therefore of the Greeks as have erected two temples to the deity of this name, have, in my opinion, acted very wisely; to the Olympian Hercules they offer sacrifice as to an immortal being; to the other they pay the rites of an hero.

45. Among the many preposterous fables current in Greece, the one concerning Hercules is not the least ridiculous. He arrived, they say, in Egypt, where the inhabitants bound him with the sacred fillet, and the usual ornaments of a victim, and made preparations to sacrifice him to Jupiter. For a while he restrained himself, but upon his being conducted with the usual solemnities to the altar, he exerted his strength, and put all his opponents to death. This story of the Greeks demonstrates the extremest ignorance of Egyptian manners; for how can it be reasonable to suppose that a people will offer human beings in sacrifice, who will not for this purpose destroy even animals, except swine, bulls, male calves without blemish, and geese? Or how could Hercules, an individual, and, as they themselves affirm, a mortal, be able to

destroy many thousands of men? I hope, however, that what I have introduced on this subject will give no offence either to gods or heroes.

46. The Mendesians, of whom I have before spoken, refuse to sacrifice goats of either sex, out of reverence to Pan, whom their traditions assert to be one of the eight deities, whose existence preceded that of the twelve. Like the Greeks, they always represent Pan in his images with the countenance of the she-goat and the legs of the male; not that they believe this has any resemblance to his person, or that he in any respect differs from the rest of the deities; the real motive which they assign for this custom I do not choose to relate. The veneration of the Mendesians for these animals, and for the males in particular, is equally great and universal; this is also extended to goat-herds. There is one he-goat more particularly honoured than the rest, whose death is seriously lamented by the whole district of the Mendesians. In the Egyptian language the word Mendes is used in common for Pan and for a goat.

47. The Egyptians regard the hog as an unclean animal, and if they casually touch one they immediately plunge themselves, clothes and all, into the water. This prejudice operates to the exclusion of all swine-herds, although natives of Egypt, from the temples: with people of this description, a

connection by marriage is studiously avoided, and they are reduced to the necessity of intermarrying among those of their own profession. The only deities to whom the Egyptians offer swine are Bacchus and Luna; to these they sacrifice them when the moon is at the full, after which they eat the flesh. Why they offer swine at this particular time, and at no other, the Egyptians have a tradition among themselves, which delicacy forbids me to explain. The following is the mode in which they sacrifice this animal to Luna: as soon as it is killed, they cut off the extremity of the tail, which, with the spleen and the fat, they enclose in the caul, and burn; upon the remainder, which at any other time they would disdain, they feast at the full moon, when the sacrifice is performed. They who are poor make figures of swine with meal, which, having first baked, they offer on the altar.

48. On the day of the feast of Bacchus, at the hour of supper, every person, before the door of his house, offers a hog in sacrifice. The swine-herd of whom they purchased it is afterwards at liberty to take it away. Except this sacrifice of the swine, the Egyptians celebrate the feast of Bacchus in the same manner as the Greeks. Instead of the phalli, they have contrived certain figures of about a cubit in length, some parts of which are made to

move. These the women carry about the streets and villages, the indications of the sex being made almost as large as the rest of the body; with these, and preceded by a piper, they sing, in a long procession, the praises of Bacchus. Why one part of the image is so disproportionately large, and why they give a motion to it alone, they explain by a sacred and mysterious reason.

49. I am of opinion that Melampus, son of Amytheon, was acquainted with this ceremony. Melampus first taught the Greeks the name and the sacrifice of Bacchus, and introduced the procession of the phalli, the mysterious purport of which he did not sufficiently explain; but since his time it has received from different sages sufficient illustration. It is unquestionable, that the use of the phalli in the sacrifice of Bacchus, with the other ceremonies which the Greeks now know and practise, were first taught them by Melampus. I therefore, without hesitation, pronounce him to have been a man of wisdom, and of skill in the art of divination. Instructed by the Egyptians in various ceremonies, and particularly in those which relate to Bacchus, with some few trifling changes, he brought them into Greece. I can by no means impute to accident the resemblance which exists in the rites of Bacchus in Egypt and in Greece; in this case they would not have differed so essen-

tially from the Grecian manners, and they might have been traced to more remote antiquity; neither will I affirm that these, or that any other religious ceremonies, were borrowed of Greece by the Egyptians; I rather think that Melampus learned all these particulars which relate to the worship of Bacchus from Cadmus, and his Tyrian companions, when they came from Phœnicia to what is now called Bœotia.

50. Egypt has certainly communicated to Greece the names of almost all the gods; that they are of barbarian origin, I am convinced by my different researches. The names of Neptune and the Dioscuri I mentioned before; with these, if we except Juno, Vesta, Themis, the Graces, and the Nereids, the names of all the other deities have always been familiar in Egypt. In this instance I do but repeat the opinions of the Egyptians. Those names of which they disclaim any knowledge are all, except Neptune, of Pelasgian derivation; for their acquaintance with this deity, they are indebted to Libya, where indeed he was first of all known, and has always been greatly honoured. The Egyptians do not pay any religious ceremonies to heroes.

51. With the above, the Greeks have derived many other circumstances of religious worship from Egypt, which I shall hereafter relate; they did not, however, learn from hence, but from the

Pelasgi, to construct the figure of Mercury in a special manner, which custom was first introduced by the Athenians, and communicated from them to others. At that period the Athenians were ranked among the nations of Greece, and had the Pelasgians for their neighbours; from which incident this people also began to be esteemed as Greeks. Of the truth of this, whoever has been initiated in the Cabirian mysteries, which the Samothracians use, and which they learned of the Pelasgi, will be necessarily convinced; for the Pelasgians, before they lived near the Athenians, formerly inhabited Samothracia, and taught the people of that country their mysteries. By them the Athenians were first of all instructed to make the figure of Mercury as I have said. For this the Pelasgians have a sacred tradition, which is explained in the Samothracian mysteries.

52. The Pelasgians, as I was informed at Dodona, formerly offered all things indiscriminately to the gods. They distinguished them by no name or surname, for they were hitherto unacquainted with either; but they called them gods, which by its etymology means disposers, from observing the orderly disposition and distribution of the various parts of the universe. They learned, but not till a late period, the names of the divinities from the Egyptians, and Bacchus was the last whom they

knew. Upon this subject they afterwards consulted the oracle of Dodona, by far the most ancient oracle of Greece, and at the period of which we speak, the only one. They desired to know whether they might with propriety adopt the names which they had learned of the barbarians; and were answered that they might; they have accordingly used them ever since in their rites of sacrifice, and from the Pelasgi they were communicated to the Greeks.

53. Of the origin of each deity, whether they have all of them always existed, as also of their form, their knowledge is very recent indeed. The invention of the Grecian theogony, the names, the honours, the forms, and the functions of the deities, may with propriety be ascribed to Hesiod and to Homer, who, I believe, lived four hundred years, and not more, before myself. If I may give my opinion, the poets who are reported to have been before these, were certainly after them. What I say of the names and origin of the gods, is on the authority of the priests of Dodona; of Hesiod and of Homer I speak my own sentiments.

54. Of the two oracles of Greece and Libya, the Egyptians speak as follows: I was told by the ministers of the Theban Jupiter, that the Phœnicians had violently carried off from Thebes two priestesses, one of whom had been sold into Libya,

the other into Greece; they added that the commencement of the above oracles must be assigned to these two women. On my requesting to know their authority for these assertions, they answered, that after a long and ineffectual search after these priestesses, they had finally learned what they had told me.

55. I have related the intelligence which I gained from the priests at Thebes: the priestesses of Dodona assert that two black pigeons flew from Thebes in Egypt, one of which settled in Libya, the other among themselves; which latter, resting on the branch of a beech-tree, declared with a human voice that here by a divine appointment was to be an oracle of Jove. The inhabitants, fully impressed that this was a divine communication, instantly complied with the injunction. The dove which flew to Libya in like manner commanded the people to fix there an oracle of Ammon, which also is an oracle of Jupiter. Such was the information I received from the priestesses of Dodona, the eldest of whom was called Promenea, the second Timarete, the youngest Nicandre; the other ministers employed in the service of the temple agreed with these in every particular.

56. My opinion of the matter is this: If the Phœnicians did in reality carry away these two priestesses, and sell one to Libya, the other to

Greece, this latter must have been carried to the Thesproti, which country, though part of which is now termed Greece, was formerly called Pelasgia. That, although in a state of servitude, she erected, under the shade of a beech-tree, a sacred edifice to Jupiter, which she might very naturally be prompted to do, from the remembrance of the temple of Jupiter at Thebes, whence she was taken. Thus she instituted the oracle, and having learned the Greek language, might probably relate that by the same Phœnicians her sister was sold for a slave to Libya.

57. The name of doves was probably given them because, being strangers, the sound of their voices might, to the people of Dodona, seem to resemble the tone of those birds. When the woman, having learned the language, delivered her thoughts in words which were generally understood, the dove might be said to have spoken with a human voice. Before she had thus accomplished herself, her voice might appear like that of a dove. It certainly cannot be supposed that a dove should speak with a human voice; and the circumstance of her being black, explains to us her Egyptian origin.

58. The two oracles of Egyptian Thebes and of Dodona, have an entire resemblance to each other. The art of divination, as now practised in our temples, is thus derived from Egypt; at least the

Egyptians were the first who introduced the sacred festivals, processions, and supplications, and from them the Greeks were instructed. It is to me a sufficient testimony of this, that these religious ceremonies are in Greece but of modern date, whereas in Egypt they have been in use from the remotest antiquity.

59. In the course of the year, the Egyptians celebrate various public festivals; but the festival in honour of Diana, at the city Bubastis, is the first in dignity and importance. The second is held in honour of Isis, at the city Busiris, which is situated in the middle of the Delta, and contains the largest temple of that goddess. Isis is called in the Greek tongue, Demeter or Ceres. The solemnities of Minerva, observed at Sais, are the third in consequence; the fourth are at Heliopolis, and sacred to the sun; the fifth are those of Latona, at Butos; the next those of Mars, solemnised at Papremis.

60. They who meet to celebrate the festival at Bubastis embark in vessels, a great number of men and women promiscuously mixed. During the passage some of the women strike their tabors, accompanied by the men playing on flutes. The rest of both sexes clap their hands, and join in chorus. Whatever city they approach, the vessels are brought to shore: of the women, some continue

their instrumental music, others call aloud to the females of the place, provoke them by injurious language, dance about, and indecently throw aside their garments. This they do at every place near which they pass. On their arrival at Bubastis, the feast commences by the sacrifice of many victims, and upon this occasion a greater quantity of wine is consumed than in all the rest of the year. The natives report that at this solemnity seven hundred thousand men and women assemble, not to mention children.

61. I have before related in what manner the rites of Isis are celebrated at Busiris. After the ceremonies of sacrifice, the whole assembly, to the amount of many thousands, flagellate themselves, but in whose honour they do this I am not at liberty to disclose. The Carians of Egypt treat themselves at this solemnity with still more severity: for they cut themselves in the face with swords, and thus distinguish themselves from the Egyptian natives.

62. At the sacrifice solemnised at Sais, the assembly is held by night; they suspend before their houses in the open air, lamps which are filled with oil mixed with salt; a wick floats at the top, which will burn all night. The feast itself is called the feast of lamps. Such of the Egyptians as do not attend the ceremony think themselves obliged

to observe the evening of the festival, and in like manner burn lamps before their houses; thus on this night, not Sais only, but all Egypt is illuminated. A religious motive is assigned for the festival itself, and for the illuminations by which it is distinguished.

63. At Heliopolis and Butos sacrifices alone are offered, but at Papremis, as at other places, in addition to the offering of victims, other religious ceremonies are observed. At the close of the day, a small number of priests crowd round the statue of Mars; a great number, armed with clubs, place themselves at the entrance of the temple. Opposite to these may be seen more than a thousand men tumultuously assembled, with clubs also in their hands, to perform their religious vows. The day before the festival they remove the statue of the god, which is kept in a small case decorated with gold, to a different apartment. The priests attendant upon the statue place it, together with its case, on a four-wheeled carriage, and begin to draw it along. Those at the entrance of the temple endeavour to prevent its admission, but the votaries above mentioned come to the succour of the god, and a combat ensues between the two parties, in which many heads are broken, and I should suppose many lives lost, though this the Egyptians positively deny.

64. The motive for this ceremony is thus explained by the natives of the country:—This temple, they say, was the residence of the mother of Mars; the god himself, who had been brought up at a distance from his parent, on his arrival at man's estate, came hither to visit his mother. The attendants, who had never seen him before, not only refused to admit him, but roughly drove him from the place. Obtaining proper assistance, he returned, severely chastised those who had opposed him, and obtained admission to his mother. From this circumstance the above mode of fighting was ever after practised on the festival of Mars, and these people were also the first who made it a point of religion not to communicate with a woman in a temple, nor enter any consecrated place after such communication without having first washed. Except the Egyptians and the Greeks, all other nations without scruple unite themselves with women in their temples, nor think it necessary to wash themselves after such communication, previous to their paying their devotions. In this instance they rank man indiscriminately with other animals, for observing that birds as well as beasts couple in shrines and temples, they conclude that it cannot be offensive to the deity. Such a mode of reasoning does not by any means obtain my approbation.

65. The superstition of the Egyptians is conspicuous in various instances, but in this more particularly, notwithstanding the vicinity of their country to Libya, the number of beasts is comparatively small, but all of them, both those which are wild and those which are domestic, are regarded as sacred. If I were to explain the reason of this prejudice, I should be led to the discussion of those sacred subjects which I particularly wish to avoid, and which, but from necessity, I should not have discussed so fully as I have. Their laws compel them to cherish animals; a certain number of men and women are appointed to this office, which is esteemed so honourable, that it descends in succession from father to son. In the presence of these animals, the inhabitants of the cities perform their vows. They address themselves as supplicants to the divinity, who is supposed to be represented by the animal in whose presence they are. They then cut off their children's hair, sometimes the whole of it, sometimes half, at other times only a third part; this they weigh in a balance against a piece of silver; as soon as the silver preponderates, they give it to the woman who keeps the beast, she in return feeds the beast with pieces of fish, which is their constant food. It is a capital offence designedly to kill any one of these animals; to destroy one accidentally is punished by a fine,

determined by the priests; but whoever, however involuntarily, kills an ibis or an hawk, cannot by any means escape death.

66. The number of domestic animals in Egypt is very great, and would be much greater if the increase of cats were not thus prevented. The female cats, when delivered of their young, carefully avoid the company of the males, who to obtain further attention from them, contrive and execute this stratagem. They steal the young from the mother, which they destroy, but do not eat. This animal, which is very fond of its young, from its desire to have more, again covets the company of the male. In every accident of fire, the cats seem to be actuated by some supernatural impulse, for the Egyptians surrounding the place which is burning, appear to be occupied with no thought but that of preserving their cats. These, however, by stealing between the legs of the spectators, or by leaping over their heads, endeavour to dart into the flames. This circumstance, whenever it happens, diffuses universal sorrow. In whatever family a cat by accident happens to die, every individual cuts off his eyebrows; but on the death of a dog they shave their heads and every part of their bodies.

67. The cats, when dead, are carried to sacred buildings, and after being salted are buried in the

city Bubastis. Of the canine species, the females are buried in consecrated chests, wherever they may happen to die, which ceremony is also observed with respect to the ichneumons. The shrew-mice and hawks are always removed to Butos; the ibis to Hermopolis; the bears, an animal rarely seen in Egypt, and the wolves, which are not much bigger than foxes, are buried in whatever place they die.

68. I proceed now to describe the nature of the crocodile, which during the four severer months of winter eats nothing. It is a quadruped, but amphibious; it is also oviparous, and deposits its eggs in the sand; the greater part of the day it spends on shore, but all the night in the water, as being warmer than the external air, whose cold is increased by the dew. No animal that I have seen or known, from being at first so remarkably diminutive, grows to so vast a size. The eggs are not larger than those of geese. On leaving the shell the young is proportionately small, but when arrived at its full size it is sometimes more than seventeen cubits in length. It has eyes like a hog, teeth large and prominent in proportion to the dimensions of its body, but, unlike all other animals, it has no tongue. It is further and most singularly distinguished, by only moving its upper jaw. Its feet are armed with strong fangs; the

skin is protected by hard scales regularly divided. In the open air its sight is remarkably acute, but it cannot see at all in the water. Living in the water its throat is always full of leeches; beasts and birds universally avoid it, the trochilus alone excepted, which, from a sense of gratitude, it treats with kindness. When the crocodile leaves the water, it reclines itself on the sand, and generally towards the west, with its mouth open. The trochilus entering its throat destroys the leeches, in acknowledgment for which service it never does the trochilus injury.

69. This animal by many of the Egyptians, is esteemed sacred, by others it is treated as an enemy. They who live near Thebes, and the lake Mœris, hold the crocodile in religious veneration. They select one which they render tame and docile, suspending golden ornaments from its ears, and sometimes gems of value; the fore feet are secured by a chain. They feed it with the flesh of the sacred victims, and with other appointed food. While it lives they treat it with unceasing attention, and when it dies, it is first embalmed, and afterwards deposited in a sacred chest. They who live in or near Elephantine, so far from considering these beasts as sacred, make them an article of food. They call them not crocodiles, but champsæ. The name of crocodiles was first im-

posed by the Ionians, from their resemblance to lizards so named by them, which are produced in the hedges.

70. Among the various methods that are used to take the crocodile, I shall only relate one which most deserves attention. They fix a piece of swine's flesh on a hook, and suffer it to float into the middle of the stream; on the banks they have a live hog, which they beat till it cries out. The crocodile hearing the noise makes towards it, and in the way encounters and devours the bait. They then draw it on shore, and the first thing they do is to fill its eyes with clay; it is thus easily manageable, which it otherwise would not be.

71. The hippopotamus is esteemed sacred in the district of Papremis, but in no other part of Egypt. I shall describe its nature and properties: it is a quadruped, its feet are cloven, and it has hoofs like an ox; the nose is short, but turned up, the teeth prominent; it resembles a horse in its mane, its tail, and its voice; it is of the size of a very large ox, and has a skin so remarkably thick, that when dried it is made into offensive weapons.

72. The Nile also produces otters, which the Egyptians venerate, as they also do the fish called lepidotus, and the eel; these are sacred to the Nile, as among the birds is one called the chenalopex.

73. They have also another sacred bird, which, except in a picture, I have never seen; it is called the phœnix. It is very uncommon, even among themselves; for according to the Heliopolitans, it comes there but once in the course of five hundred years, and then only at the decease of the parent bird. If it bear any resemblance to its picture, the wings are partly of a gold and partly of a crimson colour, and its form and size are perfectly like the eagle. They relate one thing of it which surpasses all credibility; they say that it comes from Arabia to the temple of the sun, bearing the dead body of its parent, enclosed in myrrh, which it buries. It makes a ball of myrrh, shaped like an egg, as large as it is able to carry, which it proves by experiment. This done, it excavates the mass, into which it introduces the body of the dead bird; it again closes the aperture with myrrh, and the whole becomes the same weight as when composed entirely of myrrh; it then proceeds to Egypt to the temple of the sun.

74. In the vicinity of Thebes there are also sacred serpents, not at all troublesome to men; they are very small, but have two horns on the top of the head. When they die they are buried in the temple of Jupiter, to whom they are said to belong.

75. There is a place in Arabia, near the city

Butos, which I visited for the purpose of obtaining information concerning the winged serpent. I here saw a prodigious quantity of serpents' bones and ribs, placed on heaps of different heights. The place itself is a strait betwixt two mountains, it opens upon a wide plain, which communicates with Egypt. They affirm that in the commencement of every spring, these winged serpents fly from Arabia towards Egypt, but that the ibis here meets and destroys them. The Arabians say, that in acknowledgment of this service the Egyptians hold the ibis in great reverence, which is not contradicted by that people.

76. One species of the ibis is entirely black, its beak remarkably crooked, its legs as large as those of a crane, and in size it resembles the crex : this is the enemy of the serpents. The second species is the most common; these have the head and the whole of the neck naked; the plumage is white except that on the head, the neck, the extremities of the wings, and the tail; these are of a deep black colour, but the legs and the beak resemble in all respects those of the other species. The form of the flying and of the aquatic serpents is the same; the wings of the former are not feathered, but entirely like those of the bats. And thus I have finished my account of the sacred animals.

77. Those Egyptians who live in the cultivated

parts of the country are, of all I have seen, the most ingenious, being attentive to the improvement of the memory beyond the rest of mankind. To give some idea of their mode of life: for three days successively in every month they use purges, vomits, and clysters; this they do out of attention to their health, being persuaded that the diseases of the body are occasioned by the different elements received as food. Besides this, we may venture to assert, that after the Africans there is no people in health and constitution to be compared with the Egyptians. To this advantage the climate, which is here subject to no variation, may essentially contribute; changes of all kinds, and those in particular of the seasons, promote and occasion the maladies of the body. To their bread, which they make with spelt, they give the name of cyllestis; they have no vines in the country, but they drink a liquor fermented from barley; they live principally upon fish, either salted or dried in the sun; they eat also quails, ducks, and some smaller birds, without other preparation than first salting them; but they roast and boil such other birds and fishes as they have, excepting those which are preserved for sacred purposes.

78. At the entertainments of the rich, just as the company is about to rise from the repast, a small coffin is carried round, containing a perfect

representation of a dead body : it is in size sometimes of one, but never of more than two cubits; and as it is shown to the guests in rotation, the bearer exclaims : "Cast your eyes on this figure, after death you yourself will resemble it; drink then, and be happy." Such are the customs they observe at entertainments.

79. They contentedly adhere to the customs of their ancestors, and are averse to foreign manners. Among other things which claim our approbation, they have a song, which is also used in Phœnicia, Cyprus, and other places, where it is differently named. Of all the things which astonished me in Egypt, nothing more perplexed me than my curiosity to know whence the Egyptians learned this song, so entirely resembling the Linus of the Greeks; it is of the remotest antiquity among them, and they call it Maneros. They have a tradition that Maneros was the only son of their first monarch; and that having prematurely died, they instituted these melancholy strains in his honour, constituting their first, and in earlier times, their only song.

80. The Egyptians surpass all the Greeks, the Lacedæmonians excepted, in the reverence which they pay to age : if a young person meet his senior, he instantly turns aside to make way for him; if a senior enter an apartment, the youth always rise

from their seats; this ceremony is observed by no other of the Greeks. When the Egyptians meet they do not speak, but make a profound reverence, bowing with the hand down to the knee.

81. Their habit, which they call calasiris, is made of linen, and fringed at the bottom; over this they throw a kind of shawl made of white wool, but in these vests of wool they are forbidden by their religion either to be buried or to enter any sacred edifice; this is a peculiarity of those ceremonies which are called Orphic and Pythagorean: whoever has been initiated in these mysteries can never be interred in a vest of wool, for which a sacred reason is assigned.

82. Of the Egyptians it is farther memorable, that they first imagined what month or day was to be consecrated to each deity; they also, from observing the days of nativity, venture to predict the particular circumstances of a man's life and death: this is done by the poets of Greece, but the Egyptians have certainly discovered more things that are wonderful than all the rest of mankind. Whenever any prodigy occurs, they commit the particulars to writing, and mark the events which follow it: if they afterwards observe any similar incident, they conclude that the result will be similar also.

83. The art of divination in Egypt is confined

to certain of their deities. There are in this country oracles of Hercules, of Apollo, of Minerva and Diana, of Mars, and of Jupiter; but the oracle of Latona at Butos is held in greater estimation than any of the rest: the oracular communication is regulated by no fixed system, but is differently obtained in different places.

84. The art of medicine in Egypt is thus exercised: one physician is confined to one disease; there are, of course, a great number who practise this art; some attend to disorders of the eyes, others to those of the head; some take care of the teeth, others are conversant with all diseases of the bowels; whilst many attend to the cure of maladies which are less conspicuous.

85. With respect to their funerals and ceremonies of mourning: whenever a man of any importance dies, the females of his family, disfiguring their heads and faces with dirt, leave the corpse in the house, and run publicly about, accompanied by their female relations, with their garments in disorder, their breasts exposed, and beating themselves severely: the men on their part do the same, after which the body is carried to the embalmers.

86. There are certain persons appointed by law to the exercise of this profession. When a dead body is brought to them, they exhibit to the

friends of the deceased different models highly finished in wood. The most perfect of these they say resembles one whom I do not think it religious to name in such a matter; the second is of less price, and inferior in point of execution; another is still more mean; they then inquire after which model the deceased shall be represented: when the price is determined, the relations retire, and the embalmers thus proceed. In the most perfect specimens of their art, they draw the brain through the nostrils, partly with a piece of crooked iron, and partly by the infusion of drugs; they then, with an Ethiopian stone, make an incision in the side, through which they extract the intestines; these they cleanse thoroughly, washing them with palm-wine, and afterwards covering them with pounded aromatics: they then fill the body with powder of pure myrrh, cassia, and other perfumes, except frankincense. Having sewn up the body, it is covered with nitre for the space of seventy days, which time they may not exceed; at the end of this period it is washed, closely wrapped in bandages of cotton, dipped in a gum which the Egyptians use as glue: it is then returned to the relations, who enclose the body in a case of wood, made to resemble a human figure, and place it against the wall in the repository of their dead. The above is the most costly mode of embalming.

87. They who wish to be less expensive, adopt the following method: they neither draw out the intestines, nor make any incision in the dead body, but inject an unguent made from the cedar; after taking proper means to secure the injected oil within the body, it is covered with nitre for the time above specified: on the last day they withdraw the liquor before introduced, which brings with it all the bowels and intestines; the nitre eats away the flesh, and the skin and bones only remain: the body is returned in this state, and no further care taken concerning it.

88. There is a third mode of embalming appropriated to the poor. A particular kind of ablution is made to pass through the body, which is afterwards left in nitre for the above seventy days, and then returned.

89. The wives of men of rank, and such females as have been distinguished by their beauty or importance, are not immediately on their decease delivered to the embalmers: they are usually kept for three or four days, which is done to prevent any indecency being offered to their bodies. An instance once occurred of an embalmer having made such a precaution necessary: the crime was divulged by a fellow artist.

90. If an Egyptian, or a foreigner, be found either destroyed by a crocodile, or drowned in the

water, the city nearest which the body is discovered is obliged to embalm and pay it every respectful attention, and afterwards deposit it in some consecrated place: no friend or relation is suffered to interfere, the whole process is conducted by the priests of the Nile, who bury it themselves with a respect to which a lifeless corpse would hardly seem entitled.

91. To the customs of Greece they express aversion, and, to say the truth, to those of all other nations. This remark applies, with only one exception, to every part of Egypt. Chemmis is a place of considerable note in the Thebaid, it is near Neapolis, and remarkable for a temple of Perseus the son of Danae. This temple is of a square figure, and surrounded with palm-trees. The vestibule, which is very spacious, is constructed of stone, and on the summit are placed two large marble statues. Within the consecrated inclosure stand the shrine and statue of Perseus, who, as the inhabitants affirm, often appears in the country and the temple. They sometimes find one of his sandals, which are of the length of two cubits, and whenever this happens fertility reigns throughout Egypt. Public games, after the manner of the Greeks, are celebrated in his honour. Upon this occasion they have every variety of gymnastic exercise. The rewards of

the conquerors are cattle, vests, and skins. I was once induced to inquire why Perseus made his appearance to them alone, and why they were distinguished from the rest of Egypt by the celebration of gymnastic exercises? They informed me in return that Perseus was a native of their country, as were also Danaus and Lynceus, who made a voyage into Greece, and from whom, in regular succession, they related that Perseus was descended. This hero visited Egypt for the purpose, as the Greeks also affirm, of carrying from Africa the Gorgon's head. Happening to come among them, he saw and was known to his relations. The name of Chemmis he had previously known from his mother, and he himself instituted the games which they continued to celebrate.

92. These which I have described, are the manners of those Egyptians who live in the higher parts of the country. They who inhabit the marshy grounds differ in no material instance. Like the Greeks, they confine themselves to one wife. To procure themselves the means of sustenance more easily, they make use of the following expedient: when the waters have risen to their extremest height, and all their fields are overflowed, there appears above the surface an immense quantity of plants of the lily species, which the Egyptians call the lotos; having cut down these they dry them in

the sun. The seed of the flower, which resembles that of the poppy, they bake, and make into a kind of bread; they also eat the root of this plant, which is round, of an agreeable flavour, and about the size of an apple. There is a second species of the lotos which grows in the Nile, and which is not unlike a rose. The fruit which grows from the the bottom of the root is like a wasp's nest: it is found to contain a number of kernels of the size of an olive-stone, which are very grateful, either fresh or dried. Of the byblus, which is an annual plant, after taking it from a marshy place where it grows, they cut off the tops, and apply them to various uses. They eat or sell what remains, which is nearly a cubit in length. To make this a still greater delicacy, there are many who previously roast it. With a considerable part of this people, fish continues the principal article of food; they dry it in the sun, and eat it without other preparation.

93. Those fishes which are gregarious, seldom multiply in the Nile; they usually propagate in the lakes. At the season of spawning they move in vast multitudes towards the sea; the males lead the way, and emit the engendering principle in their passage; this the females absorb as they follow, and in consequence, conceive. As soon as the seminal matter has had its proper operation, they leave the

sea, return up the river, and endeavour to regain their accustomed haunts. The mode, however, of their passage is reversed, the females lead the way, whilst the males follow. The females do now what the males did before, they drop their spawn, resembling small grains of millet, which the males eagerly devour. Every particle of this contains a small fish, and each which escapes the males regularly increases till it becomes a fish. Of these fish, such as are taken in their passage towards the sea, are observed to have the left part of their heads depressed, which on their return is observed of their right. The cause of this is obvious: as they pass to the sea they rub themselves against the banks on the left side; as they return they keep closely to the same bank, and in both instances press against it that they may not be obliged to deviate from their course by the current of the stream. As the Nile gradually rises, the water first fills those cavities of the land which are nearest the river. As soon as these are saturated, an abundance of small fry may be discovered. The cause of their increase may perhaps be thus explained: when the Nile ebbs, the fish, which in the preceding season had deposited their spawn in the mud, retreat reluctantly with the stream; but at the proper season, when the river flows, this spawn is matured into fish.

94. The inhabitants of the marshy grounds make use of an oil, which they term the kiki, expressed from the Sillicyprian plant. In Greece this plant springs spontaneously without any cultivation, but the Egyptians sow it on the banks of the river and of the canals; it there produces fruit in great abundance, but of a very strong odour: when gathered, they obtain from it, either by friction or pressure, an unctuous liquid, which diffuses an offensive smell, but for burning it is equal in quality to the oil of olives.

95. The Egyptians are provided with a remedy against gnats of which there are a surprising number. As the wind will not suffer these insects to rise far from the ground, the inhabitants of the higher part of the country usually sleep in turrets. They who live in the marshy grounds use this substitute: each person has a net, with which they fish by day, and which they render useful by night. They cover their beds with their nets, and sleep securely beneath them. If they slept in their common habits, or under-linen, the gnats would not fail to torment them, which they do not even attempt through a net.

96. Their vessels of burden are constructed of a species of thorn, which resembles the lotos of Cyrene, and which distils a gum. From this thorn they cut planks, about two cubits square: after

disposing these in the form of bricks, and securing them strongly together, they place from side to side benches for the rowers. They do not use timber artificially carved, but bend the planks together with the bark of the byblus made into ropes. They have one rudder, which goes through the keel of the vessel; their mast is made of the same thorn, and the sails are formed from the byblus. These vessels are hauled along by land, for unless the wind be very favourable they can make no way against the stream. When they go with the current, they throw from the head of the vessel a hurdle made of tamarisk, fastened together with reeds; they have also a perforated stone of the weight of two talents: this is let fall at the stern secured by a rope. The name of this kind of bark is baris, which the above hurdle, impelled by the tide, draws swiftly along. The stone at the stern regulates its motion. They have immense numbers of these vessels, and some of them of the burden of many thousand talents.

97. During the inundation of the Nile, the cities only are left conspicuous, appearing above the waters like the islands of the Ægean Sea. As long as the flood continues, vessels do not confine themselves to the channel of the river, but traverse the fields and the plains. They who then go from Naucratis to Memphis, pass by the pyramids; this, however, is not the usual course, which lies through the

point of the Delta and the city of Cercasorus. If from the sea and the town of Canopus, the traveller desires to go by the plains to Naucratis he must pass by Anthilla and Archandros.

98. Of these places Anthilla is the most considerable : whoever may be sovereign of Egypt, it is assigned perpetually as part of the revenues of the queen, and appropriated to the particular purpose of providing her with sandals; this has been observed ever since Egypt was tributary to Persia. I should suppose that the other city derives its name from Archander, the son of Pthius, son-in-law of Danaus, and grandson of Achæus. There may probably have been some other Archander, for the name is certainly not Egyptian.

99. All that I have hitherto asserted has been the result of my own personal remarks or diligent inquiry. I shall now proceed to relate what I learned from conversing with Egyptians, to which I shall occasionally add that I myself have witnessed.—Menes, the first sovereign of Egypt as I was informed by the priests, effectually detached the ground on which Memphis stands from the water. Before his time the river flowed entirely along the sandy mountain on the side of Libya. But this prince, by constructing a bank at the distance of a hundred stadia from Memphis, towards the south, diverted the course of the Nile, and led

it, by means of a new canal, through the centre of the mountains. Even at this present period under the dominion of the Persians this artificial channel is annually repaired and regularly preserved. If the river were here once to break its banks, the whole town of Memphis would be greatly endangered. It was the same Menes who, upon the solid ground thus rescued from the water, first built the town now known by the name of Memphis, which is situate in the narrowest part of Egypt. To the north and west of Memphis, he also sank a lake, communicating with the river, which, from the situation of the Nile, it was not possible to effect towards the east. He moreover erected on the same spot a magnificent temple in honour of Vulcan.

100. The priests afterwards recited to me from a book the names of three hundred and thirty sovereigns (successors of Menes); in this continued series eighteen were Ethiopians, and one a female native of the country, all the rest were men and Egyptians. The female was called Nitocris, which was also the name of the Babylonian princess. They affirm that the Egyptians having slain her brother, who was their sovereign, she was appointed his successor; and that afterwards, to avenge his death, she destroyed by artifice a great number of Egyptians. By her orders a large subterraneous

apartment was constructed, professedly for festivals, but in reality for a different purpose. She invited to this place a great number of those Egyptians whom she knew to be the principal instruments of her brother's death, and then by a private canal introduced the river amongst them. They added that, to avoid the indignation of the people, she suffocated herself in an apartment filled with ashes.

101. None of [these monarchs, as my informers related, were distinguished by any acts of magnificence or renown, except Mœris, who was the last of them. Of this prince various monuments remain. He built the north entrance of the temple of Vulcan, and sank a lake, the dimensions of which I shall hereafter describe. Near this he also erected pyramids, whose magnitude, when I speak of the lake, I shall particularise. These are lasting monuments of his fame; but as none of the preceding princes performed anything memorable, I shall pass them by in silence.

102. The name of Sesostris, who lived after these monarchs, claims our attention. According to the priests, he was the first who, passing the Arabian Gulf in a fleet of long vessels, reduced under his authority the inhabitants bordering on the Erythrean Sea. He proceeded yet farther, till he came to a sea which, on account of the number of shoals, was not navigable. On his return to Egypt, as I

learned from the same authority, he levied a mighty army, and made a martial progress by land, subduing all the nations whom he met with on his march. Whenever he was opposed by a people who proved themselves brave, and who discovered an ardour for liberty, he erected columns in their country, upon which he inscribed his own name and that of his nation, and how he had here conquered by the force of his arms; but where he met with little or no opposition, upon similar columns which he erected he added indications of the female sex, expressive of the pusillanimity of the people.

103. Continuing his progress, he passed over from Asia to Europe, and subdued the countries of Scythia and Thrace. Here I believe he stopped, for monuments of his victory are discovered thus far, but no farther. On his return, he came to the river Phasis; but I am by no means certain whether he left a detachment of his forces as a colony in this district, or whether some of his men, fatigued with their laborious service, remained here of their own accord.

104. The Colchians certainly appear to be of Egyptian origin, which, indeed, before I had conversed with any one on the subject, I had always believed. But as I was desirous of being satisfied, I interrogated the people of both countries. The

result was, that the Colchians seemed to have better remembrance of the Egyptians than the Egyptians had of the Colchians. The Egyptians were of opinion that the Colchians were descended from part of the troops of Sesostris. To this I myself was also inclined, because they are black, and have short and curling hair; which latter circumstance may not, however, be insisted upon as evidence, because it is common to many other nations. But a second and better argument is, that the inhabitants of Colchos, Egypt, and Ethiopia are the only people who from time immemorial have used circumcision. The Phœnicians and the Syrians of Palestine acknowledge that they borrowed this custom from Egypt. Those Syrians who live near the rivers Thermodon and Parthenius, and their neighbours the Macrones, confess that they learned it, and that too in modern times, from the Colchians. These are the only people who use circumcision, and who use it precisely like the Egyptians. As this practice can be traced both in Egypt and Ethiopia to the remotest antiquity, it is not possible to say who first introduced it. The Egyptians certainly communicated it to the other nations by means of their commercial intercourse. The Phœnicians, who are connected with Greece, do not any longer imitate the Egyptians in this particular, their male children not being circumcised.

105. But the Colchians have another mark of resemblance to the Egyptians. Their manufacture of linen is alike, and peculiar to those two nations; they have similar manners, and the same language. The linen which comes from Colchis the Greeks call Sardonian; the linen of Egypt, Egyptian.

106. The greater part of the pillars which Sesostris erected in the places which he conquered are no longer to be found. Some of them I myself have seen in Palestine of Syria, with an emblem derived from sex, and with the inscriptions which I have before mentioned. In Ionia there are two figures of this king formed out of a rock; one is in the road from Ephesus to Phocæa, the other betwixt Sardis and Smyrna. Both of them represent a man, five palms in height; the right hand holds a javelin, the left a bow; the rest of the armour is partly Egyptian and partly Ethiopian. Across his breast, from shoulder to shoulder, there is this inscription in the sacred characters of Egypt: "I conquered this country by the force of my arms." Who the person here represented is, or of what country, is not specified; both are told elsewhere. Some have been induced, on examination, to pronounce this to be the figure of Memnon, but they must certainly be mistaken.

107. The same priests informed me that Sesostris returned to Egypt with an immense number of

captives of the different nations which he had conquered. On his arrival at the Pelusian Daphne, his brother, to whom he had confided the government in his absence, invited him and his family to take up their abode with him, which, when they had done, he surrounded their apartments with combustibles, and set fire to the building. As soon as Sesostris discovered the villany, he deliberated with his wife, who happened to be with him, what measures to pursue. She advised him to place two of their six children across the parts which were burning, that they might serve as a bridge for the preservation of themselves and of the rest. This Sesostris executed. Two of the children consequently perished; the remainder were saved with their father.

108. Sesostris did not omit to avenge himself on his brother. On his return to Egypt he employed the captives of the different nations he had vanquished to collect those immense stones which were employed in the temple of Vulcan. They were also compelled to make those vast and numerous canals by which Egypt is intersected. In consequence of their involuntary labours, Egypt, which was before conveniently adapted to those who travelled on horseback or in carriages, became unfit for both. The canals occur so often, and in so many winding directions, that to travel on horseback is disagree-

able, but in carriages impossible. The prince, however, was influenced by a patriotic motive. Before his time those who inhabited the inland parts of the country, at a distance from the river, on the ebbing of the Nile, suffered great distress from the want of water, of which they had none but from muddy wells.

109. The same authority informed me that Sesostris made a regular distribution of the lands of Egypt. He assigned to each Egyptian a square piece of ground, and his revenues were drawn from the rent, which every individual annually paid him. Whoever was a sufferer by the inundation of the Nile, was permitted to make the king acquainted with his loss. Certain officers were appointed to inquire into the particulars of the injury, that no man might be taxed beyond his ability. It may not be improbable to suppose that this was the origin of geometry, and that the Greeks learned it from hence. As to the pole, the gnomon, and the division of the day into twelve parts, the Greeks received them from the Babylonians.

110. Except Sesostris, no monarch of Egypt was ever master of Ethiopia. This prince placed as a monument some marble statues before the temple of Vulcan; two of these were thirty cubits in height, and represented him and his queen; four

others, of twenty cubits each, represented his four children. A long time afterwards, Darius, King of Persia, was desirous of placing before these a statue of himself, but the high priest of Vulcan violently opposed it, urging that the actions of Darius were far less splendid than those of the Egyptian Sesostris. This latter prince had vanquished as many nations as Darius, and had also subdued the Scythians, who had never yielded to the arms of Darius. Therefore, says he, it can never be just to place before the statues of Sesostris the figure of a prince whose exploits have not been equally illustrious. They told me that Darius forgave this remonstrance.

111. On the death of Sesostris, his son Pheron, as the priests informed me, succeeded to his throne. This prince undertook no military expedition; but by the action I am going to relate he lost the use of his eyes. When the Nile was at its extreme height of eighteen cubits, and had overflowed the fields, a sudden wind arose, which made the waters impetuously swell. At this juncture the prince hurled a javelin into the vortex of the stream; he was in a moment deprived of sight, and continued blind for the space of ten years; in the eleventh, an oracle was communicated to him from Butos, intimating that the period of his punishment was expired, and that he should recover his sight by

washing his eyes with the water of a woman who had never known any man but her husband. Pheron first made the experiment with his own wife, and when this did not succeed he applied water of other women indiscriminately. Having at length recovered his sight, he assembled all the women, except her whose fidelity had removed his calamity, in a city which is to this day called Erythrebolos; all these, with the town itself, he destroyed by fire, but he married the woman who had deserved his gratitude. On his recovery he sent magnificent presents to all the more celebrated temples; to that of the Sun he sent two obelisks, too remarkable to be unnoticed; each was formed of one solid stone, one hundred cubits high, and eight broad.

112. The successor of Pheron, as the same priests informed me, was a citizen of Memphis, whose name in the Greek tongue was Proteus. His shrine is still to be seen at Memphis; it is situated to the south of the temple of Vulcan, and is very magnificently decorated. The Phœnicians of Tyre dwell in its vicinity, and, indeed, the whole of the place is denominated the Tyrian camp. In this spot, consecrated to Proteus, there is also a small temple, dedicated to Venus the Stranger; this Venus I conjecture is no other than Helen, the daughter of Tyndaris, because she, I was told,

resided for some time at the court of Proteus, and because this building is dedicated to Venus the Stranger; no other temple of Venus is distinguished by this appellation.

113. To my inquiries on the subject of Helen, these priests answered as follows: Paris having carried off Helen from Sparta, was returning home, but meeting with contrary winds in the Ægean, he was driven into the Egyptian sea. As the winds continued unfavourable, he proceeded to Egypt, and was driven to the Canopian mouth of the Nile, and to Tarichea; in this place was a temple of Hercules, which still remains; if any slave fled to this for refuge, and in testimony of his consecrating himself to the service of the god, submitted to be marked with certain sacred characters, no one was suffered to molest him. This custom has been strictly observed, from its first institution to the present period. The servants of Paris, aware of the privileges of this temple, fled thither from their master, and with the view of injuring Paris, became the suppliants of the divinity. They published many accusations against their master, disclosing the whole affair of Helen, and the wrong done to Menelaus; this they did, not only in the presence of the priests, but also before Thonis, the governor of the district.

114. Thonis instantly dispatched a messenger

to Memphis, with orders to say thus to Proteus: "There is arrived here a Trojan, who has perpetrated an atrocious crime in Greece; he has seduced the wife of his host, and has carried her away, with a great quantity of treasure; adverse winds have forced him hither; shall I suffer him to depart without molestation, or shall I seize his person and property?" The answer which Proteus sent was thus conceived: "Whoever that man is, who has violated the rites of hospitality, seize and bring him before me, that I may examine him."

115. Thonis upon this seized Paris, and detaining his vessels, instantly sent him to Proteus, with Helen and all his wealth; on their arrival, Proteus inquired of Paris who he was, and whence he came: Paris faithfully related the name of his family and country, and from whence he last set sail. But when Proteus proceeded to make enquiries concerning Helen, and how he obtained possession of her person, Paris hesitated in his answers; his slaves who had deserted him, explained and proved the particulars of his guilt, in consequence of which Proteus made this determination: "If I did not esteem it a very heinous crime to put any stranger to death, whom unfavourable winds have driven to my coast, I would assuredly, thou most abandoned man, avenge that Greek

whose hospitality thou hast treacherously violated. Thou hast not only seduced his wife, but having violently taken her away, still criminally detainest her; and, as if this were not enough, thou hast robbed and plundered him! But as I can by no means prevail upon myself to put a stranger to death, I shall suffer you to depart; the woman and your wealth I shall detain, till the Greek himself thinks proper to demand her. Do you and your companions depart within three days from my coasts, or expect to be treated as enemies."

116. Thus, according to the narrative of the priests, did Helen come to the court of Proteus. I conceive that this circumstance could not be unknown to Homer; but as he thought it less ornamental to his poem, he forbore to use it. That he actually did know it is evident from that part of the Iliad where he describes the voyage of Paris; this evidence he has nowhere retracted. He informs us that Paris, after various wanderings, at length arrived at Sidon, in Phœnicia; it is in the "Bravery of Diomed"; the passage is this:

> There lay the vestures of no vulgar art,
> Sidonian maids embroidered every part;
> When from soft Sidon youthful Paris bore,
> With Helen touching on the Tyrian shore.
> Il. vi. 390.

He again introduces this subject in the "Odyssey":

> These drugs, so friendly to the joys of life,
> Bright Helen learned from Thone's imperial wife:
> Who swayed the sceptre where prolific Nile
> With various simples clothes the fattened soil.
> With wholesome herbage mixed, the direful bane
> Of vegetable venom taints the plain.
>
> Od. iv. 315.

Menelaus also says thus to Telemachus:

> Long on the Egyptian coast by calms confined,
> Heaven to my fleet refused a prosperous wind:
> No vows had we preferred, nor victim slain,
> For this the gods each favouring gale restrain.
>
> Od. iv. 473.

In these passages Homer confesses himself acquainted with the voyage of Paris to Egypt, for Syria borders upon Egypt, and the Phœnicians, to whom Sidon belongs, inhabit part of Syria.

117. The last passage of these confirms sufficiently the argument which may be deduced from the former, that the Cyprian verses were never written by Homer. These relate that Paris, in company with Helen, assisted by a favourable wind and sea, passed in three days from Sparta to Troy; on the contrary, it is asserted in the Iliad, that Paris, after carrying away Helen, wandered about to various places. But enough of Homer and the Cyprian verses.

118. On my desiring to know of the same priests whether what the Greeks affirm concerning Troy

was true or false, they told me the following particulars, which they assured me they received from Menelaus himself. After the loss of Helen, the Greeks assembled in great numbers at Teucris to assist Menelaus; they disembarked and encamped; they then dispatched ambassadors to Troy, whom Menelaus himself accompanied. On their arrival they made a formal demand of Helen, and of the wealth which Paris had at the same time clandestinely taken, as well as general satisfaction for the injury. The Trojans then and afterwards uniformly persisted in declaring, that they had among them neither the person nor the wealth of Helen, but that both were in Egypt, and they thought it hard that they should be made responsible for what Proteus, king of Egypt, certainly possessed. The Greeks, believing themselves deluded, laid siege to Troy, and persevered till they took it. But when Helen was not to be found in the captured town, and the same assertions concerning her were continued, they at length obtained credit, and Menelaus himself was dispatched to Proteus.

119. As soon as he arrived in Egypt he proceeded up the Nile to Memphis. On his relating the object of his journey, he was honourably entertained; Helen, who had been treated with respect, was restored to him, and with her, all his treasures. Inattentive to these acts of kindness, Menelaus

perpetrated a great enormity against the Egyptians; the winds preventing his departure, he took two children of the people of the country, and with great barbarity offered them in sacrifice. As soon as the circumstance was known, universal indignation was excited against him, and he was pursued, but he fled by sea into Africa, and the Egyptians could trace him no further. Of the above facts, some they knew, as having happened among themselves, and others were the result of much diligent inquiry.

120. This intelligence concerning Helen I received from the Egyptian priests, to which I am inclined to add, as my opinion, that if Helen had been actually in Troy they would certainly have restored her to the Greeks, with or without the consent of Paris. Priam and his connections could never have been so infatuated, as to endanger the preservation of themselves and their children, merely that Paris might have Helen ; but even if such had been their determination at first, still after having lost in their different contests with the Greeks many of their countrymen, and among these, if the poets may be believed, several of their king's own sons, I cannot imagine but that Priam, even if he had married her himself, would have restored Helen, if no other means had existed of averting these calamities. We may add to this, that Paris was not the immediate heir

to the crown, for Hector was his superior both in age and valour; Paris, therefore, could not have possessed any remarkable influence in the State, neither would Hector have countenanced the misconduct of his brother, from which he himself, and the rest of his countrymen, had experienced so many and such great calamities. But the restoration of Helen was not in their power, and the Greeks placed no dependence on their assertions, which were indisputably true; but all this, with the subsequent destruction of Troy, might be ordained by Providence, to instruct mankind that the gods proportioned punishments to crimes.

121. The same instructors farther told me that Proteus was succeeded by Rhampsinitus; he built the west entrance of the temple of Vulcan; in the same situation he also erected two statues, twenty-five cubits in height. That which faces the north the Egyptians call Summer, the one to the south Winter; this latter is treated with no manner of respect, but they worship the former, and make offerings before it. This prince possessed such abundance of wealth that, far from surpassing, none of his successors ever equalled him in affluence. For the security of his riches he constructed a stone edifice, connected with his palace by a wall. The man whom he employed so artfully disposed one of the stones, with a dishonest view, that two or even

one person might remove it from its place. In this building, when completed, the king deposited his treasures. Some time afterwards, the artist found his end approaching, and having two sons, he called them both before him, and informed them in what manner, with a view to their future emolument and prosperity, he had built the king's treasury. He then explained the particular circumstance and situation of the stone, gave them minutely its dimensions, by observance of which they might become the managers of the king's riches. On the death of the father, the sons were not long before they availed themselves of their secret. Under the advantage of the night, they visited the building, discovered and removed the stone, and carried away with them a large sum of money. As soon as the king entered the apartment, he saw the vessels which contained his money materially diminished; he was astonished beyond measure, for as the seals were unbroken, and every entrance properly secured, he could not possibly direct his suspicion against any one. This was several times repeated; the thieves continued their visits, and the king as regularly saw his money decrease. To effect a discovery, he ordered some traps to be placed round the vessels which contained his riches. The robbers came as before; one of them proceeding as usual directly to the vessels, was caught in the snare : as soon as he was sensible of his situation, he called his brother, and acquainted him with it; he withal entreated him to cut off his head without a moment's delay, as the only means of preventing his own detection and consequent loss of life ; he approved and obeyed his advice, and replacing properly the stone, he returned home with the head of his brother. As soon as it was light the king entered the apartment, and seeing the body secured in the snare without a head, the building in no part disturbed, nor the smallest appearance of any one having been there, he was more astonished than ever. In this perplexity he commanded the body to be hanged from the wall, and having stationed guards on the spot, he directed them to seize and bring before him whoever should discover any symptoms of compassion or sorrow at sight of the deceased. The mother being much exasperated at this exposure of her son, threatened the surviving brother that if he did not contrive and execute some means of removing the body, she would immediately go to the king and disclose all the circumstances of the robbery. The young man in vain endeavoured to alter the woman's determination; he therefore put in practice the following expedient :—He got together some asses, which he loaded with flasks of wine ; he then drove them near the place where the guards were stationed to watch the body of his brother; as soon as he approached, he secretly removed the pegs from the mouths of two or three of the skins, and when he saw the wine running about, he began to beat his head, and to cry out vehemently, with much pretended confusion and distress. The soldiers, perceiving the accident, instantly ran with vessels, and such wine as they were able to catch they considered as so much gain to themselves. At first, with great apparent anger, he reproached and abused them, but he gradually listened to their endeavours to console and pacify him; he then proceeded at leisure to turn his asses out of the road, and to secure his flasks. He soon entered into conversation with the guards, and affecting to be pleased with the drollery of one of them, he gave them a flask of wine; they accordingly sat down to drink, and insisted upon his bearing them company: he complied with their solicitations, and a second flask was presently the effect of their civility to him. The wine had soon its effect, the guards became exceedingly drunk, and fell fast asleep; under the advantage of the night, the young man took down the body of his brother, and in derision shaved the right cheeks of the guards; he placed the body on one of the asses, and returned home, having thus satisfied his mother. When the king heard of what had happened he was enraged beyond measure; but still determined on the detection of the criminal, he contrived this, which to me seems a most improbable part of the story:—He commanded his daughter to offer her person indiscriminately to every comer, upon condition that, before she did so, each should tell her the most artful as well as the most wicked thing he had ever done; if any one should disclose the circumstance of which he wished to be informed, she was to seize him, and prevent his escape. The daughter obeyed the injunction of her father; the thief, knowing what was intended, prepared still farther to disappoint and deceive the king. He cut off the arm near the shoulder from his brother's recently dead body, and, concealing it under his cloak, he visited the king's daughter; when he was asked the same question as the rest, he replied, "That the most wicked thing he had ever done was the cutting off the head of his brother, who was caught in a snare in the king's treasury; the most artful thing was his making the guards drunk, and by that means effecting the removal of his brother's body." On hearing this she endeavoured to apprehend him, but he, favoured by the night, put out to her the dead arm, which she seizing was thus deluded, whilst he made his escape. On hearing this also, the king was equally astonished at the art and audacity of the man; he was afterwards induced to make a proclamation through the different parts of his dominions, that if the offender would appear before him, he would not only pardon, but liberally reward him. The thief, trusting to his word, appeared: Rhampsinitus was delighted with the man, and thinking his ingenuity beyond all parallel, gave him his daughter. The king conceived the Egyptians superior in subtlety to all the world, but he thought this man superior even to the Egyptians.

122. After this event, they told me that the same king descended alive beneath the earth, to what the Greeks call the infernal regions, where he played at dice with the goddess Ceres, and alternately won and lost. On his return she presented him with a napkin embroidered with gold. This period of his return was observed by the Egyptians as a solemn festival, and has continued to the time of my remembrance; whether the above, or some other incident, was the occasion of this feast, I will not take upon me to determine. The ministers of this solemnity have a vest woven within the space of the day; this is worn by a priest whose eyes are covered with a bandage. They conduct him to the path which leads to the temple of Ceres, and there leave him. They assert that two wolves meet the priest thus blinded, and lead him

to the temple, though at the distance of twenty stadia from the city, and afterwards conduct him back again to the place where they found him.

123. Every reader must determine for himself with respect to the credibility of what I have related; for my own part I heard these things from the Egyptians, and think it necessary to transcribe the result of my inquiries. The Egyptians esteem Ceres and Bacchus as the great deities of the realms below; they are also the first of mankind who have defended the immortality of the soul. They believe that on the dissolution of the body the soul immediately enters some other animal, and that, after using as vehicles every species of terrestrial, aquatic, and winged creatures, it finally enters a second time into a human body. They affirm that it undergoes all these changes in the space of three thousand years. This opinion some amongst the Greeks have at different periods of time adopted as their own; but I shall not, though I am able, specify their names.

124. I was also informed by the same priests that, till the reign of Rhampsinitus, Egypt was not only remarkable for its abundance, but for its excellent laws. Cheops, who succeeded this prince, degenerated into the extremest profligacy of conduct. He barred the avenues to every temple, and

forbade the Egyptians to offer sacrifices. He proceeded next to make them labour servilely for himself. Some he compelled to hew stones in the quarries of the Arabian mountains, and drag them to the banks of the Nile; others were appointed to receive them in vessels, and transport them to a mountain of Libya. For this service an hundred thousand men were employed, who were relieved every three months. Ten years were consumed in the hard labour of forming the road through which these stones were to be drawn; a work, in my estimation, of no less fatigue and difficulty than the pyramid itself. This causeway is five stadia in length, forty cubits wide, and its extreme height thirty-two cubits, the whole is of polished marble, adorned with the figures of animals. Ten years, as I remarked, were exhausted in forming this causeway, not to mention the time employed in the vaults of the hill upon which the pyramids are erected. These he intended as a place of burial for himself, and were in an island which he formed by introducing the waters of the Nile. The pyramid itself was a work of twenty years. It is of a square form; every front is eight plethra long, and as many in height; the stones very skilfully cemented, and none of them of less dimensions than thirty feet.

125. The ascent of the pyramid was regularly

graduated by what some call steps, and others altars. Having finished the first flight, they elevated the stones to the second by the aid of machines constructed of short pieces of wood; from the second, by a similar engine, they were raised to the third, and so on to the summit. Thus there were as many machines as there were regular divisions in the ascent of the pyramid, though in fact there might only be one, which, being easily manageable, might be removed from one range of the building to another as often as occasion made it necessary. Both modes have been told me, and I know not which best deserves credit. The summit of the pyramid was first of all finished; descending thence, they regularly completed the whole. Upon the outside were inscribed, in Egyptian characters, the various sums of money expended, in the progress of the work, for the radishes, onions, and garlic consumed by the artificers. This, as I well remember, my interpreter informed me, amounted to no less a sum than one thousand six hundred talents. If this be true, how much more must it have necessarily cost for iron tools, food, and clothes for the workmen, particularly when we consider the length of time they were employed on the building itself, adding what was spent in the hewing and conveyance of the stones, and the construction of the subterraneous apartments?

126. Cheops having exhausted his wealth, was so flagitious, that he degraded his daughter, commanding her to make the most of her opportunities. She complied with her father's injunctions, but I was not told what sum she thus procured: at the same time she took care to perpetuate the memory of herself; with which view she solicited every one of her lovers to present her with a stone. With these it is reported the middle of the three pyramids, fronting the larger one, was constructed, the elevation of which on each side is one hundred and fifty feet.

127. According to the Egyptians, this Cheops reigned fifty years. His brother Chephren succeeded to his throne, and adopted a similar conduct. He also built a pyramid, but this was less than his brother's, for I measured them both; it has no subterraneous chambers, nor any channel for the admission of the Nile, which in the other pyramid surrounds an island, where the body of Cheops is said to be deposited. Of this latter pyramid, the first ascent is entirely of Ethiopian marble of divers colours, but it is not so high as the larger pyramid, near which it stands, by forty feet. This Chephren reigned fifty-six years; the pyramid he built stands on the same hill with that erected by his brother: the hill itself is near one hundred feet high.

128. Thus for the space of one hundred and

six years the Egyptians were exposed to every species of oppression and calamity, not having in all this period permission to worship in their temples. They have so extreme an aversion for the memory of these two monarchs, that they are not very willing to mention their names. They call their pyramids by the name of the shepherd Philitis, who at that time fed his cattle in those places.

129. Mycerinus, the son of Cheops, succeeded Chephren: as he evidently disapproved of his father's conduct, he commanded the temples to be opened, and the people, who had been reduced to the extremest affliction, were again permitted to offer sacrifice, at the shrines of their gods. He excelled all that went before him in his administration of justice. The Egyptians revere his memory beyond that of all his predecessors, not only for the equity of his decisions, but because, if complaint was ever made of his conduct as a judge, he condescended to remove and redress the injury. Whilst Mycerinus thus distinguished himself by his exemplary conduct to his subjects, he lost his daughter and only child, the first misfortune he experienced. Her death excessively afflicted him: and wishing to honour her funeral with more than ordinary splendour, he enclosed her body in an heifer made of wood, and richly ornamented with gold.

130. This heifer was not buried; it remained even to my time, in the palace of Sais, placed in a superb hall. Every day, costly aromatics were burnt before it, and every night it was splendidly illuminated; in an adjoining apartment are deposited statues of the different concubines of Mycerinus, as the priests of Sais informed me. These are to the number of twenty; they are colossal figures, made of wood, and in a naked state, but what women they are intended to represent I presume not to say: I merely relate what I was told.

131. Of this heifer, and these colossal figures, there are some who speak thus: Mycerinus, they say, conceived an unnatural passion for his daughter, and treated her with criminal violence. She having, in the anguish of her mind, strangled herself, her father buried her in the manner we have described. The mother cut off the hands of those female attendants who assisted the king in his designs upon his daughter, and therefore these figures are marked by the same imperfections as distinguished the persons they represent when alive. The whole of this story, and that in particular which relates to the hands of these figures, to me seems very preposterous. I myself saw the hands lying on the ground, merely, as I thought, from the effect of time.

132. The body of this heifer is covered with a purple cloth, whilst the head and neck are very richly gilt: betwixt the horns there is a golden star; it is made to recline on its knees, and is about the size of a large cow. Every year it is brought from its apartment; at the period when the Egyptians flagellate themselves in honour of a certain god, whom it does not become me to name, this heifer is produced to the light: it was the request, they say, of the dying princess to her father, that she might once every year behold the sun.

133. Mycerinus, after the loss of his daughter, met with a second calamity: an oracle from the city Butos informed him that he should live six years, but die in the seventh; the intelligence astonished him, and he sent a message in return to reproach the goddess with injustice; for that his father and his uncle, who had been injurious to mankind, and impious to the gods, had enjoyed each a length of life of which he was to be deprived who was distinguished for his piety. The reply of the oracle told him that his early death was the consequence of the conduct for which he commended himself; he had not fulfilled the purpose of the Fates, who had decreed that for the space of one hundred and fifty years Egypt should be oppressed; of which determination the two

preceding monarchs had been aware, but he had not. As soon as Mycerinus knew that his destiny was immutable, he caused an immense number of lamps to be made, by the light of which, when evening approached, he passed his hours in the festivity of the banquet: he frequented by day and by night the groves and streams, and whatever places he thought productive of delight: by this method of changing night into day, and apparently multiplying his six years into twelve, he thought to convict the oracle of falsehood.

134. This prince also built a pyramid, but it was not by twenty feet so high as his father's; it was a regular square on every side, three hundred feet in height, and as far as the middle of Ethiopian stone. Some of the Greeks erroneously believe this to have been erected by Rhodopis, the courtesan, but they do not seem to me even to know who this Rhodopis was; if they had they never could have ascribed to her the building of a pyramid, produced at the expense of several thousand talents: besides this, Rhodopis lived at a different period, in the time, not of Mycerinus, but of Amasis, and many years after the monarchs who erected the pyramids. Rhodopis was born in Thrace, the slave of Iadmon, the son of Hephæstopolis the Samian: she was the fellow-servant of Æsop, who wrote fables, and was also the slave of

Iadmon; all which may be thus easily proved: The Delphians, in compliance with the directions of the oracle, had desired publicly to know if any one required atonement to be made for the death of Æsop; but none appeared to do this, except a grandson of Iadmon, bearing the same name.

135. Rhodopis was first carried to Egypt by Xanthus of Samos, whose view was to make money by her shame. Her liberty was purchased for an immense sum by Charaxus of Mytilene, son of Scamandronymus, and brother of Sappho, the poetess: thus becoming free, she afterwards continued in Egypt, where her beauty procured her considerable wealth, though by no means adequate to the construction of such a pyramid; the tenth part of her riches whoever pleases may even now ascertain, and they will not be found so great as has been represented. Wishing to perpetuate her name in Greece, she contrived what had never before been imagined, as an offering for the Delphic temple: she ordered a tenth part of her property to be expended in making a number of iron spits, each large enough to roast an ox; they were sent to Delphi, where they are now to be seen behind the altar presented by the Chians. The courtesans of Naucratis are generally beautiful; she of whom we speak was so universally celebrated that her name is familiar to every Greek.

There was also another courtesan, named Archidice, well known in Greece, though of less repute than Rhodopis. Charaxus, after giving Rhodopis her liberty, returned to Mytilene: this woman was severely handled by Sappho in some satirical verses. But enough has been said on the subject of Rhodopis.

136. After Mycerinus, as the priests informed me, Asychis reigned in Egypt; he erected the east entrance to the temple of Vulcan, which is far the greatest and most magnificent. Each of the above-mentioned vestibules is elegantly adorned with figures well carved, and other ornaments of buildings, but this is superior to them all. In this reign, when commerce was checked and injured, from the extreme want of money, an ordinance passed that any one might borrow money, giving the body of his father as a pledge: by this law the sepulchre of the debtor became in the power of the creditor; for if the debt was not discharged, he could neither be buried with his family, nor in any other vault, nor was he suffered to inter one of his descendants. This prince, desirous of surpassing all his predecessors, left as a monument of his fame a pyramid of brick, with this inscription on a piece of marble : "Do not disparage my worth by comparing me to those pyramids composed of stone; I am as much superior to them as Jove is to the rest of the

deities; I am formed of bricks, which were made of mud adhering to poles drawn from the bottom of the lake." This was the most memorable of this king's actions.

137. He was succeeded by an inhabitant of Anysis, whose name was Anysis, and who was blind. In his reign, Sabacus, King of Ethiopia, overran Egypt with a numerous army; Anysis fled to the morasses, and saved his life, but Sabacus continued master of Egypt for the space of fifty years. Whilst he retained his authority, he made it a rule not to punish any crime with death, but according to the magnitude of the offence he condemned the criminal to raise the ground near the place to which he belonged; by which means the situation of the different cities became more and more elevated: they were somewhat raised under the reign of Sesostris, by the digging of the canals, but they became still more so under the reign of the Ethiopian. This was the case with all the cities of Egypt, but more particularly with the city of Bubastis. There is in this city a temple which well deserves our attention; there may be others larger as well as more splendid, but none which have a more delightful situation. Bubastis in Greek is synonymous with Artemis or Diana.

138. This temple, taking away the entrance, forms an island; two branches of the Nile meet at

the entrance of the temple, and then separating, flow on each side entirely round it; each of these branches is one hundred feet wide, and regularly shaded with trees; the vestibule is forty cubits high, and ornamented with various figures, none of which are less than six cubits. The temple is in the centre of the town, and is in every part a conspicuous object; its situation has never been altered, though every other part of the city has been elevated; a wall ornamented with sculpture surrounds the building; in the interior part, a grove of lofty trees shades the temple, in the centre of which is the statue of the goddess: the length and breadth of the temple each way is one stadium. There is a paved way which leads through the public square of the city, from the entrance of this temple to that of Mercury, which is about thirty stadia in length.

139. The deliverance of Egypt from the Ethiopian was, as they told me, effected by a vision, which induced him to leave the country: a person appeared to him in a dream, advising him to assemble all the priests of Egypt, and afterwards cut them in pieces. This vision to him seemed to demonstrate that in consequence of some act of impiety, which he was thus tempted to perpetrate, his ruin was at hand, from Heaven or from man. Determined not to do this deed, he

conceived it more prudent to withdraw himself, particularly as the time of his reigning over Egypt was, according to the declarations of the oracles, now to terminate. During his former residence in Ethiopia, the oracles of his country had told him that he should reign fifty years over Egypt: this period being accomplished, he was so terrified by the vision, that he voluntarily withdrew himself.

140. Immediately on his departure from Egypt, the blind prince quitted his place of refuge, and resumed the government: he had resided for the period of fifty years in a solitary island, which he himself had formed of ashes and of earth. He directed those Egyptians who frequented his neighbourhood for the purpose of disposing of their corn, to bring with them, unknown to their Ethiopian master, ashes for his use. Amyrtæus was the first person who discovered this island, which all the princes who reigned during the space of five hundred years before Amyrtæus were unable to do: it is called Elbo, and is on each side ten stadia in length.

141. The successor of this prince was Sethos, a priest of Vulcan; he treated the military of Egypt with extreme contempt, and as if he had no occasion for their services. Among other indignities, he deprived them of their aruræ, or fields of fifty feet square, which, by way of reward, his prede-

cessors had given to each soldier: the result was, that when Sennacherib, King of Arabia and Assyria, attacked Egypt with a mighty army, the warriors, whom he had thus treated, refused to assist him. In this perplexity the priest retired to the shrine of his god, before which he lamented his danger and misfortunes: here he sank into a profound sleep, and his deity promised him in a dream that if he marched to meet the Assyrians he should experience no injury, for that he would furnish him with assistance. The vision inspired him with confidence; he put himself at the head of his adherents, and marched to Pelusium, the entrance of Egypt: not a soldier accompanied the party, which was entirely composed of tradesmen and artisans. On their arrival at Pelusium, so immense a number of mice infested by night the enemy's camp, that their quivers and bows, together with what secured their shields to their arms, were gnawed in pieces. In the morning the Arabians, finding themselves without arms, fled in confusion, and lost great numbers of their men. There is now to be seen in the temple of Vulcan, a marble statue of this king having a mouse in his hand, and with this inscription: "Whoever thou art, learn, from my fortune, to reverence the gods."

142. Thus, according to the information of the Egyptians and their priests, from the first king to

this last, who was priest of Vulcan, a period of three hundred and forty-one generations had passed, in which there had been as many high priests, and the same number of kings. Three generations are equal to one hundred years, and, therefore, three hundred generations are the same as ten thousand years; the forty-one generations that remain make one thousand three hundred and forty years. During the above space of eleven thousand three hundred and forty years, they assert that no divinity appeared in a human form; but they do not say the same of the time anterior to this account, or of that of the kings who reigned afterwards. During the above period of time the sun, they told me, had four times deviated from his ordinary course, having twice risen where he uniformly goes down, and twice gone down where he uniformly rises. This, however, had produced no alteration in the climate of Egypt; the fruits of the earth, and the phenomena of the Nile, had always been the same, nor had any extraordinary or fatal diseases occurred.

143. When the historian Hecatæus was at Thebes, he recited to the priests of Jupiter the particulars of his descent, and endeavoured to prove that he was the sixteenth in a right line from some god. · But they did to him what they afterwards did to me, who had said nothing on

the subject of my family. They introduced me into a spacious temple, and displayed to me a number of figures in wood; this number I have before specified, for every high priest places here during his life a wooden figure of himself. The priests enumerated them before me, and proved, as they ascended from the last to the first, that the son followed the father in regular succession. When Hecatæus, in the explanation of his genealogy, ascended regularly, and traced his descent in the sixteenth line from a god, they opposed a similar mode of reasoning to his, and absolutely denied the possibility of a human being's descent from a god. They informed him that each of these colossal figures was a Piromis, descended from a Piromis; and they further asserted, that without any variation this had uniformly occurred to the number of the three hundred and forty-one, but in this whole series there was no reference either to a god or a hero. Piromis, in the Egyptian language, means one "beautiful and good."

144. From these priests I learned that the individuals whom these figures represented, so far from possessing any divine attributes, had all been what I have described. But in the times which preceded immortal beings had reigned in Egypt, that they had communication with men, and had uniformly one superior; that Orus, whom the

Greeks call Apollo, was the last of these; he was the son of Osiris, and, after he had expelled Typhon, himself succeeded to the throne; it is also to be observed that in the Greek tongue Osiris is synonymous with Bacchus.

145. The Greeks consider Hercules, Bacchus, and Pan as the youngest of their deities; but Egypt esteems Pan as the most ancient of the gods, and even of those eight who are accounted the first. Hercules was among those of the second rank in point of antiquity, and one of those called the twelve gods. Bacchus was of the third rank, and among those whom the twelve produced. I have before specified the number of years which the Egyptians reckon from the time of Hercules to the reign of Amasis; from the time of Pan a still more distant period is reckoned; from Bacchus, the youngest of all, to the time of Amasis, is a period, they say, of fifteen thousand years. On this subject the Egyptians have no doubts, for they profess to have always computed the years, and to have kept written accounts of them with the minutest accuracy. From Bacchus, who is said to be the son of Semele, the daughter of Cadmus, to the present time, is one thousand six hundred years; from Hercules, the reputed son of Alcmena, is nine hundred years; and from Pan, whom the Greeks call the son of Penelope and Mercury, is

eight hundred years, before which time was the Trojan war.

146. Upon this subject I have given my own opinion, leaving it to my readers to determine for themselves. If these deities had been known in Greece, and then grown old, like Hercules the son of Amphitryon, Bacchus the son of Semele, and Pan the son of Penelope, it might have been asserted of them that although mortals, they possessed the names of those deities known in Greece in the times which preceded. The Greeks affirm of Bacchus, that as soon as he was born Jove enclosed him in his thigh, and carried him to Nysa, a town of Ethiopia beyond Egypt: with regard to the nativity of Pan they have no tradition among them; from all which, I am convinced, that these deities were the last known among the Greeks, and that they date the period of their nativity from the precise time that their names came amongst them; the Egyptians are of the same opinion.

147. I shall now give some account of the internal history of Egypt; to what I learned from the natives themselves, and the information of strangers, I shall add what I myself beheld. At the death of their sovereign, the priest of Vulcan, the Egyptians recovered their freedom; but as they could not live without kings, they chose twelve, among whom they divided the different districts of

Egypt. These princes connected themselves with each other by inter-marriages, engaging solemnly to promote their common interest, and never to engage in any acts of separate policy. The principal motive of their union was to guard against the declaration of an oracle, which had said, that whoever among them should offer in the temple of Vulcan a libation from a brazen vessel should be sole sovereign of Egypt; and it is to be remembered that they assembled indifferently in every temple.

148. It was the resolution of them all, to leave behind them a common monument of their fame. With this view, beyond the lake Mœris, near the city of crocodiles, they constructed a labyrinth, which exceeds, I can truly say, all that has been said of it; whoever will take the trouble to compare them, will find all the works of Greece much inferior to this, both in regard to the workmanship and expense. The temples of Ephesus and Samos may justly claim admiration, and the pyramids may individually be compared to many of the magnificent structures of Greece, but even these are inferior to the labyrinth. It is composed of twelve courts, all of which are covered; their entrances are opposite to each other, six to the north and six to the south; one wall encloses the whole; the apartments are of two kinds, there are fifteen hundred above the surface of the ground,

and as many beneath, in all three thousand. Of the former I speak from my own knowledge and observation; of the latter, from the information I received. The Egyptians who had the care of the subterraneous apartments would not suffer me to see them, and the reason they alleged was, that in these were preserved the sacred crocodiles, and the bodies of the kings who constructed the labyrinth: of these therefore I presume not to speak; but the upper apartments I myself examined, and I pronounce them among the greatest efforts of human industry and art. The almost infinite number of winding passages through the different courts excited my warmest admiration: from spacious halls I passed through smaller apartments, and from them again to large and magnificent courts, almost without end. The ceilings and walls are all of marble, the latter richly adorned with the finest sculpture; around each court are pillars of the whitest and most polished marble: at the point where the labyrinth terminates stands a pyramid one hundred and sixty cubits high, having large figures of animals engraved on its outside, and the entrance to it is by a subterraneous path.

149. Wonderful as this labyrinth is, the lake Mœris, near which it stands, is still more extraordinary: the circumference of this is three thousand six hundred stadia, or sixty schœni, which

is the length of Egypt about the coast. This lake stretches itself from north to south, and in its deepest parts is two hundred cubits; it is entirely the produce of human industry, which indeed the work itself testifies, for in its centre may be seen two pyramids, each of which is two hundred cubits above and as many beneath the water; upon the summit of each is a colossal statue of marble, in a sitting attitude. The precise altitude of these pyramids is consequently four hundred cubits; these four hundred cubits, or one hundred orgyiæ, are adapted to a stadium of six hundred feet; an orgyia is six feet, or four cubits, for a foot is four palms, and a cubit six.

The waters of the lake are not supplied by springs; the ground which it occupies is of itself remarkably dry, but it communicates by a secret channel with the Nile; for six months the lake empties itself into the Nile, and the remaining six the Nile supplies the lake. During the six months in which the waters of the lake ebb, the fishery which is here carried on furnishes the royal treasury with a talent of silver every day; but as soon as the Nile begins to pour its waters into the lake, it produces no more than twenty minæ.

150. The inhabitants affirm of this lake, that it has a subterraneous passage inclining inland towards the west, to the mountains above Memphis,

where it discharges itself into the Libyan sands. I was anxious to know what became of the earth, which must somewhere have necessarily been heaped up in digging this lake; as my search after it was fruitless, I made inquiries concerning it of those who lived nearer the lake. I was the more willing to believe them when they told me where it was carried, as I had before heard of a similar expedient used at Nineveh, an Assyrian city. Some robbers, who were solicitous to get possession of the immense treasures of Sardanapalus, King of Nineveh, which were deposited in subterraneous apartments, began from the place where they lived to dig underground, in a direction towards them. Having taken the most accurate measurement, they continued their mine to the palace of the king; as night approached they regularly emptied the earth into the Tigris, which flows near Nineveh, and at length accomplished their purpose. A plan entirely similar was executed in Egypt, except that the work was here carried on, not by night, but by day; the Egyptians threw the earth into the Nile, as they dug it from the trench; thus it was regularly dispersed, and this, as they told me, was the process of the lake's formation.

151. These twelve kings were eminent for the justice of their administration. Upon a certain occasion they were offering sacrifice in the temple

of Vulcan, and on the last day of the festival were about to make the accustomed libation; for this purpose the chief priest handed to them the golden cups used on these solemnities, but he mistook the number, and, instead of twelve, gave only eleven. Psammitichus, who was the last of them, not having a cup, took off his helmet, which happened to be of brass, and from this poured his libation. The other princes wore helmets in common, and had them on the present occasion, so that the circumstance of this one king having and using his was accidental and innocent. Observing, however, this action of Psammitichus, they remembered the prediction of the oracle, "that he among them who should pour a libation from a brazen vessel should be sole monarch of Egypt." They minutely investigated the matter, and being satisfied that this action of Psammitichus was entirely the effect of accident, they could not think him worthy of death; they nevertheless deprived him of a considerable part of his power, and confined him to the marshy parts of the country, forbidding him to leave this situation, or to communicate with the rest of Egypt.

152. This Psammitichus had formerly fled to Syria from Sabacus, the Ethiopian, who had killed his father Necos; when the Ethiopian, terrified by the vision, had abandoned his dominions, those

Egyptians who lived near Sais had solicited Psammitichus to return. He was now a second time driven into exile amongst the fens by the eleven kings, from this circumstance of the brazen helmet He felt the strongest resentment for the injury, and determined to avenge himself on his persecutors; he sent therefore to the oracle of Latona, at Butos, which has among the Egyptians the highest character for veracity. He was informed that the sea should avenge his cause by producing brazen figures of men. He was little inclined to believe that such a circumstance could ever occur; but, some time afterwards, a body of Ionians and Carians, who had been engaged in a voyage of plunder, were compelled by distress to touch at Egypt; they landed in brazen armour. Some Egyptians hastened to inform Psammitichus in his marshes of this incident; and as the messenger had never before seen persons so armed, he said that some brazen men had arisen from the sea, and were plundering the country. He instantly conceived this to be the accomplishment of the oracle's prediction, and entered into alliance with the strangers, engaging them by splendid promises to assist him. With them and his Egyptian adherents he vanquished the eleven kings.

153. After he thus became sole sovereign of Egypt, he built at Memphis the vestibule of the

temple of Vulcan, which is towards the south; opposite to this he erected an edifice for Apis, in which he is kept when publicly exhibited. It is supported by colossal figures twelve cubits high, which serve as columns; the whole of the building is richly decorated with sculpture. Apis, in the language of Greece, is Epaphus.

154. In acknowledgment of the assistance he had received, Psammitichus conferred on the Ionians and Carians certain lands, which were termed the Camp, immediately opposite to each other, and separated by the Nile; he fulfilled also his other engagements with them, and entrusted to their care some Egyptian children, to be instructed in the Greek language, from whom come those who, in Egypt, act as interpreters. This district, which is near the sea, somewhat below Bubastis, at the Pelusian mouth of the Nile, was inhabited by the Ionians and Carians for a considerable time. At a succeeding period Amasis, to avail himself of their assistance against the Egyptians, removed them to Memphis. Since the time of their first settlement in Egypt, they have preserved a constant communication with Greece, so that we have a perfect knowledge of Egyptian affairs from the reign of Psammitichus. They were the first foreigners whom the Egyptians received among them: within my remembrance, in the places

which they formerly occupied, the docks for their ships, and vestiges of their buildings, might be seen.

155. Of the Egyptian oracle I have spoken already, but it so well deserves attention, that I shall expatiate still farther on the subject. It is sacred to Latona, and, as I have before said, in a large city called Butos, at the Sebennitic mouth of the Nile, as approached from the sea. In this city stands a temple of Apollo and Diana; that of Latona, whence the oracular communications are made, is very magnificent, having porticoes forty cubits high. What most excited my admiration was the shrine of the goddess; it was of one solid stone, having equal sides; the length of each was forty cubits; the roof is of another solid stone, no less than four cubits in thickness.

156. Of all the things which here excite attention this shrine is, in my opinion, the most to be admired. Next to this is the island of Chemmis, which is near the temple of Latona, and stands in a deep and spacious lake; the Egyptians affirm it to be a floating island. I did not witness the fact, and was astonished to hear that such a thing existed. In this island is a large edifice sacred to Apollo, having three altars and surrounded by palms, the natural produce of the soil. There are also great varieties of other plants, some of which

produce fruit, others are barren. The Egyptians thus explain the circumstance of this island's floating: it was once fixed and immovable, when Latona, who has ever been esteemed one of the eight primary divinities, dwelt at Butos. Having received Apollo in trust from Isis, she consecrated and preserved him in this island, which, according to their account, now floats. This happened when Typhon, earnestly endeavouring to discover the son of Osiris, came hither. Their tradition says that Apollo and Diana were the offspring of Bacchus and Isis, and that Latona was their nurse and preserver. Apollo, Ceres, and Diana the Egyptians respectively call Orus, Isis, and Bubastis. From this alone Æschylus, son of Euphorion, the first poet who represented Diana as the daughter of Ceres, took his account, and referred to this incident the circumstance of the island's floating.

157. Psammitichus reigned in Egypt fifty-four years, twenty-nine of which he consumed in the siege of a great city of Syria, which he afterwards took; the name of this place was Azotus. I know not that any town ever sustained so long and obstinate a siege.

158. Psammitichus had a son, whose name was Necos, by whom he was succeeded in his authority. This prince first commenced that canal leading to the Red Sea, which Darius, King of Persia, after-

wards continued. The length of this canal is equal to a four days' voyage, and it is wide enough to admit two triremes abreast. The water enters it from the Nile, a little above the city Bubastis: it terminated in the Erythrean Sea, not far from Patumos, an Arabian town. They began to sink this canal in that part of Egypt which is nearest Arabia. Contiguous to it is a mountain, which stretches towards Memphis, and contains quarries of stone. Commencing at the foot of this, it extends from west to east, through a considerable tract of country, and where a mountain opens to the south is discharged into the Arabian gulf. From the northern to the southern, or, as it is generally called, the Erythrean Sea, the shortest passage is over mount Cassius, which divides Egypt from Syria, from whence to the Arabian gulf are exactly a thousand stadia. The way by the canal, on account of the different circumflexions, is considerably longer. In the prosecution of this work, under Necos, no less than one hundred and twenty thousand Egyptians perished. He at length desisted from his undertaking, being admonished by an oracle that all his labour would turn to the advantage of a barbarian; and it is to be observed that the Egyptians term all barbarians who speak a language different from their own.

159. As soon as Necos discontinued his labours

with respect to the canal, he turned all his thoughts to military enterprises. He built vessels of war, both on the Northern Ocean and in that part of the Arabian gulf which is near the Erythrean Sea. Vestiges of his naval undertakings are still to be seen. His fleets were occasionally employed, but he also by land conquered the Syrians in an engagement near the town of Magdolum, and after his victory obtained possession of Cadytis, a Syrian city. The vest which he wore when he got this victory he consecrated to Apollo, and sent to the Milesian Branchidæ. After a reign of seventeen years he died, leaving the kingdom to his son Psammis.

160. During the reign of this prince some ambassadors arrived in Egypt from the Eleans. This people boasted that the establishment of the Olympic games possessed every excellence, and was not surpassed even by the Egyptians, though the wisest of mankind. On their arrival they explained the motives of their journey; in consequence of which the prince called a meeting of the wisest of his subjects. At this assembly the Eleans described the particular regulations they had established, and desired to know if the Egyptians could recommend any improvement. After some deliberation, the Egyptians inquired whether their fellow-citizens were permitted to contend at

these games. They were informed, in reply, that all the Greeks, without distinction, were suffered to contend. The Egyptians observed, that this must, of course, lead to injustice, for it was impossible not to favour their fellow-citizens in preference to strangers. If, therefore, the object of their voyage to Egypt was to render their regulations perfect, they should suffer only strangers to contend in their games, and particularly exclude the Eleans.

161. Psammis reigned but six years; he made an expedition to Ethiopia, and died soon afterwards. He was succeeded by his son Apries, who, next to his grandfather Psammitichus, was fortunate beyond all his predecessors, and reigned five-and-twenty years. He made war upon Sidon, and engaged the King of Tyre in battle by sea. I shall briefly mention in this place the calamities which afterwards befell him; but I shall discuss them more fully when I treat of the Libyan affairs. Apries having sent an army against the Cyreneans, received a severe check. The Egyptians ascribed this misfortune to his own want of conduct; and imagining themselves marked out for destruction, revolted from his authority. They supposed his views were, by destroying them, to secure his tyranny over the rest of their country. The friends, therefore, of such as had been

slain, with those who returned in safety, openly rebelled.

162. On discovery of this, Apries sent Amasis to soothe the malcontents. Whilst this officer was persuading them to desist from their purpose, an Egyptian standing behind him placed a helmet on his head, saying that by this act he made him king. The sequel proved that Amasis was not averse to the deed; for as soon as the rebels had declared him king he prepared to march against Apries; on intelligence of this event, the king sent Patarbemis, one of the most faithful of those who yet adhered to him, with directions to bring Amasis alive to his presence. Arriving where he was, he called to Amasis. Patarbemis persisted in desiring him to obey the king; Amasis replied, he had long determined to do so, and that Apries should have no reason to complain of him, for he would soon be with him, and bring others also. Patarbemis was well aware of the purport of this answer; taking, therefore, particular notice of the hostile preparations of the rebels, he returned, intending instantly to inform the king of his danger. Apries, when he saw him, without hearing him speak, as he did not bring Amasis, ordered his nose and ears to be cut off. The Egyptians of his party, incensed at this treatment of a man much and

deservedly respected, immediately went over to Amasis.

163. Apries on this put himself at the head of his Ionian and Carian auxiliaries, who were with him to the amount of thirty thousand men, and marched against the Egyptians. Departing from Sais, where he had a magnificent palace, he proceeded against his subjects; Amasis also prepared to meet his master and the foreign mercenaries. The two armies met at Momemphis, and made ready for battle.

164. The Egyptians are divided into seven classes. These are, the priests, the military, herdsmen, swincherds, tradesmen, interpreters, and pilots. They take their names from their professions. Egypt is divided into provinces, and the soldiers, from those which they inhabit, are called Calasiries and Hermotybies.

165. The Hermotybian district contains Busiris, Sais, Chemmis, Papremis, the island of Prosopis, and part of Natho: which places, at the highest calculation, furnish one hundred and sixty thousand Hermotybians. These, avoiding all mercantile employments, follow the profession of arms.

166. The Calasirians inhabit Thebes, Bubastis, Apthis, Tanis, Mendes, Sebennis, Athribis, Pharbæthis, Thmuis, Onuphis, Anysis, and Mycephoris, which is an island opposite to Bubastis. In their

most perfect state of population, these places furnish two hundred and fifty thousand men. Neither must these follow mechanic employments, but the son regularly succeeds the father in a military life.

167. I am not able to decide whether the Greeks borrowed this last-mentioned custom from the Egyptians, for I have also seen it observed in various parts of Thrace, Scythia, Persia, and Lydia. It seems, indeed, to be an established prejudice, even among nations the least refined, to consider mechanics and their descendants in the lowest rank of citizens, and to esteem those as the most noble who were of no profession, annexing the highest degrees of honour to the exercise of arms. This idea prevails throughout Greece, but more particularly at Lacedæmon; the Corinthians, however, do not hold mechanics in disesteem.

168. The soldiers and the priests are the only ranks in Egypt which are honourably distinguished; these each of them receive from the public a portion of ground of twelve aruræ, free from all taxes. Each arura contains a hundred Egyptian cubits, which are the same as so many cubits of Samos. Besides this, the military enjoy, in their turns, other advantages: one thousand Calasirians and as many Hermotybians are every year on duty as the king's guards; whilst on this

service, in addition to their assignments of land, each man has a daily allowance of five pounds of bread, two of beef, with four arusteres of wine.

169. Apries with his auxiliaries, and Amasis at the head of the Egyptians, met and fought at Momemphis. The mercenaries displayed great valour, but, being much inferior in number, were ultimately defeated. Apries is said to have entertained so high an opinion of the permanence of his authority, that he conceived it not to be in the power even of a deity to dethrone him. He was, however, conquered and taken prisoner; after his captivity he was conducted to Sais, to what was formerly his own, but then the palace of Amasis. He was here confined for some time, and treated by Amasis with much kindness and attention. But the Egyptian soon began to reproach him for preserving a person who was their common enemy, and he was induced to deliver up Apries to their power. They strangled, and afterwards buried him in the tomb of his ancestors, which stands in the temple of Minerva, on the left side of the vestibule. In this temple the inhabitants of Sais buried all the princes who were of their province, but the tomb of Amasis is more remote from the building than that of Apries and his ancestors.

170. In the area before this temple is a large marble chamber, magnificently adorned with

obelisks, in the shape of palm-trees, with various other ornaments; in this chamber is a niche with two doors, and here his body was placed. They have also at Sais the tomb of a certain personage, whom I do not think myself permitted to name. It is behind the temple of Minerva, and is continued the whole length of the wall of that building. Around this are many large obelisks, near which is a lake, whose banks are lined with stone; it is of a circular form, and, as I should think, as large as that of Delos, which is called Trochöeides.

171. Upon this lake are represented by night the accidents which happened to him whom I dare not name: the Egyptians call them their mysteries. Concerning these, at the same time that I confess myself sufficiently informed, I feel myself compelled to be silent. Of the ceremonies also in honour of Ceres, which the Greeks call Thesmophoria, I may not venture to speak, further than the obligations of religion will allow me. They were brought from Egypt by the daughters of Danäus, and by them revealed to the Pelasgian women. But when the tranquillity of the Peloponnese was disturbed by the Dorians, and the ancient inhabitants expelled, these rites were insensibly neglected or forgotten. The Arcadians, who retained their original habitations, were the only people who preserved them.

172. Such being the fate of Apries, Amasis, who was of the city of Siuph, in the district of Sais, succeeded to the throne. At the commencement of his reign, the Egyptians, remembering his plebeian origin, held him in contempt; but his mild conduct and political sagacity afterwards conciliated their affection. Among other valuables which he possessed, was a gold vessel, kept for mean uses, in which he and his guests were accustomed to spit and wash their feet: of the materials of this he made a statue of some god, which he placed in the most conspicuous part of the city. The Egyptians assembling before it, paid it divine honours: on hearing which, the king called them together, and informed them that the image they thus venerated was made of a vessel of gold, which he and they had formerly used for the most unseemly purposes. He afterwards explained to them the similar circumstances of his own fortune, who, though formerly a plebeian, was now their sovereign, and entitled to their reverence. By such means he secured their attachment, as well as their submissive obedience to his authority.

173. The same prince thus regulated his time: from the dawn of the day to such time as the public square of the city was filled with people, he gave audience to whoever required it. The rest of the

day he spent at the table, where he drank, laughed, and diverted himself with his guests, indulging in every species of licentious conversation. Upon this conduct some of his friends remonstrated :—" Sir," they observed, "do you not dishonour your rank by these excessive and unbecoming levities ? From your awful throne you ought to employ yourself in the administration of public affairs, and by such conduct increase the dignity of your name and the veneration of your subjects. Your present life is most unworthy of a king." "They," replied Amasis, "who have a bow, bend it only at the time they want it; when not in use, they suffer it to be relaxed; it would otherwise break, and not be of service when exigence required. It is precisely the same with a man; if, without some intervals of amusement, he applied himself constantly to serious pursuits, he would imperceptibly lose his vigour both of mind and body. It is the conviction of this truth which influences me in the division of my time."

174. It is asserted of this Amasis, that whilst he was in a private position he avoided every serious avocation, and gave himself entirely up to drinking and jollity. If at any time he wanted money for his expensive pleasures, he had recourse to robbery. By those who suspected him as the author of their loss, he was frequently, on his pro-

testing himself innocent, carried before the oracle, by which he was frequently condemned, and as often acquitted. As soon as he obtained the supreme authority, such deities as had pronounced him innocent he treated with the greatest contumely, neglecting their temples, and never offering them either presents or sacrifice ; this he did by way of testifying his dislike of their false declarations. Such, however, as decided on his guilt, in testimony of their truth and justice, he reverenced, as true gods, with every mark of honour and esteem.

175. This prince erected at Sais, in honour of Minerva, a magnificent portico, exceeding everything of the kind in size and grandeur. The stones of which it was composed were of a very uncommon size and quality, and decorated with a number of colossal statues and androsphynges of enormous magnitude. To repair this temple, he also collected stones of an amazing thickness, part of which he brought from the quarries of Memphis, and part from the city of Elephantine, which is distant from Sais a journey of about twenty days. But what, in my opinion, is most of all to be admired, was an edifice which he brought from Elephantine, constructed of one entire stone. The carriage of it employed two thousand men, all of whom were pilots for an entire period of three years. The length of this structure on the outside

is twenty-one cubits, it is fourteen wide, and eight high; in the inside the length of it is twenty-two cubits and twenty digits, twelve cubits wide, and five high. It is placed at the entrance of the temple. The reason it was carried no further is this: the architect, reflecting upon his long and continued fatigue, sighed deeply, which incident Amasis construed as an omen, and obliged him to desist. Some, however, affirm that one of those employed to move it by levers was crushed by it, for which reason it was advanced no farther.

176. To other temples also Amasis made many and magnificent presents. At Memphis, before the temple of Vulcan, he placed a colossal recumbent figure, which was seventy-five feet long. Upon the same pediment are two other colossal figures, formed out of the same stone, and each twenty feet high. Of the same size, and in the same attitude, another colossal statue may be seen at Sais. This prince built also at Memphis the temple of Isis, the grandeur of which excites universal admiration.

177. With respect to all those advantages which the river confers upon the soil, and the soil on the inhabitants, the reign of Amasis was auspicious to the Egyptians, who under this prince could boast of twenty thousand cities well inhabited. Amasis is further remarkable for having instituted that

law which obliges every Egyptian once in the year to explain to the chief magistrate of his district the means by which he obtains his subsistence. The refusal to comply with this ordinance, or the not being able to prove that a livelihood was procured by honest means, was a capital offence. This law Solon borrowed from Egypt, and established at Athens, where it still remains in force, experience having proved its wisdom.

178. This king was very partial to the Greeks, and favoured them upon every occasion. Such as wished to have a regular communication with Egypt, he permitted to have a settlement at Naucratis. To others, who did not require a fixed residence, as being only engaged in occasional commerce, he assigned certain places for the construction of altars, and the performance of their religious rites. The most spacious and celebrated temple which the Greeks have they call Hellenium. It was built at the joint expense of the Ionians of Chios, Teos, Phocea, and Clazomenæ; of the Dorians of Rhodes, Cnidus, Halicarnassus, and Phaselis; of the Æolians of Mitylene only. Hellenium is the common property of all these cities, who also appoint proper officers for the regulation of their commerce. The claims of other cities to these distinctions and privileges are absurd and false. The Æginetæ, it must be observed, constructed by them-

selves a temple to Jupiter, as did the Samians to Juno, and the Milesians to Apollo.

179. Formerly Naucratis was the sole emporium of Egypt; whoever came to any other than the Canopian mouth of the Nile, was compelled to swear that it was entirely accidental, and was, in the same vessel, obliged to go thither. Naucratis was held in such great estimation, that if contrary winds prevented a passage, the merchant was obliged to move his goods on board the common boats of the river, and carry them round the Delta to Naucratis.

180. By some accident the ancient temple of Delphi was once consumed by fire, and the Amphictyons voted a sum of three hundred talents to be levied for the purpose of rebuilding it. A fourth part of this was assigned to tue Delphians, who, to collect their quota, went about to different cities, and obtained a very considerable sum from Egypt. Amasis presented them with a thousand talents of alum. The Greeks who resided in Egypt made a collection of twenty minæ.

181. This king made a strict and amicable confederacy with the Cyrenians; to cement which he determined to take a wife of that country, either to show his particular attachment to the Cyrenians, or his partiality to a woman of Greece. She whom he married is reported by some to have been the

daughter of Battus, by others of Arcesiläus, or, as some say, of Critobulus. She was certainly descended of an honourable family, and her name was Ladice. When the nuptials came to be consummated, the king found himself afflicted with an imbecility which he experienced under no other circumstances. The continuance of this induced him thus to address his wife: "You have certainly practised some charm to my injury; expect not therefore to escape, but prepare to undergo the most cruel death." When the woman found all expostulations ineffectual, she vowed, in the temple of Venus, "that if on the following night her husband should find himself restored, she would present a statue to her at Cyrene." Her wishes were accomplished, and Amasis ever afterwards distinguished her by the kindest affection. Ladice performed her vow, and sent a statue to Venus; it has remained to my time, and may be seen near the city of Cyrene. This same Ladice, when Cambyses afterwards conquered Egypt, was, as soon as he discovered who she was, sent back without injury to Cyrene.

182. Numerous were the marks of liberality which Amasis bestowed on Greece. To Cyrene he sent a golden statue of Minerva, with a portrait of himself. To the temple of Minerva at Lindus he gave two marble statues, with a linen corselet,

which latter well deserves inspection. He presented two figures of himself, carved in wood, to the temple of Juno at Samos; they were placed immediately behind the gates, where they still remain. His kindness to Samos was owing to the hospitality which subsisted between him and Polycrates, the son of Æax. He had no such motive of attachment to Lindus, but was moved by the report that the temple of Minerva was erected there by the daughters of Danäus, when they fled from the sons of Ægyptus. Such was the munificence of Amasis, who was also the first person that conquered Cyprus, and compelled it to pay him tribute.

SCYTHIA DESCRIBED BY HERODOTUS.

1. DARIUS, after the capture of Babylon, undertook an expedition against Scythia. Asia was now both populous and rich, and he was desirous of avenging on the Scythians the injuries they had formerly committed by entering Media and defeating those who opposed them. During a period of twenty-eight years, the Scythians, as I have before remarked, retained the sovereignty of the Upper Asia; entering into which, when in pursuit of the Cimmerians, they expelled the Medes, its ancient possessors. After this long absence from their country, the Scythians were desirous to return, but here as great a labour awaited them as they had experienced in their expedition into Media; for the women, deprived so long of their husbands, had united themselves with their slaves, and they found a numerous body in arms ready to dispute their progress.

2. It is a custom with the Scythians to deprive all their slaves of sight on account of the milk, which is their customary drink. They have a par-

ticular kind of bone, shaped like a flute: this is applied under the tail of a mare, and blown into from the mouth. It is one man's office to blow, another's to milk the mare. Their idea is, that the veins of the animal being thus inflated, the dugs are proportionably filled. When the milk is thus obtained, they place it in deep wooden vessels, and the slaves are directed to keep it in continual agitation. Of this, that which remains at top is most esteemed; what subsides is of inferior value. This it is which induces the Scythians to deprive all their captives of sight, for they do not cultivate the ground, but lead a pastoral life.

3. From the union of these slaves with the Scythian women, a numerous progeny was born, who, when informed of their origin, readily advanced to oppose those who were returning from Media. Their first exertion was to intersect the country by a large and deep trench, which extended from the mountains of Tauris to the Palus Mæotis. They then encamped opposite to the Scythians, who were endeavouring to effect a passage. Various engagements ensued, in which the Scythians obtained no advantage. "My countrymen," at length one of them exclaimed, "what are we doing? In this contest with our slaves, every action diminishes our number, and by killing those who oppose us, the value of victory

decreases. Let us throw aside our darts and our arrows, and rush upon them only with the whips which we use for our horses. Whilst they see us with arms, they think themselves our equals in birth and importance; but as soon as they shall perceive the whip in our hands, they will be impressed with the sense of their servile condition, and resist no longer."

4. The Scythians approved the advice; their opponents forgot their former exertions and fled. In this manner the Scythians obtained the sovereignty of Asia; and thus, after having been expelled by the Medes, they returned to their country. From the above motives Darius, eager for revenge, prepared to lead an army against them.

5. The Scythians affirm of their country that it was of all others the last formed, which happened in this manner: When this region was in its original and desert state, the first inhabitant was named Targitaus, a son, as they say (but which to me seems incredible), of Jupiter, by a daughter of the Borysthenes. This Targitaus had three sons, Lipoxais, Arpoxais, and lastly Colaxais. Whilst they possessed the country, there fell from heaven into the Scythian district a plough, a yoke, an axe, and a goblet, all of gold. The eldest of the brothers was the first who saw them; who,

running to take them, was burnt by the gold. On his retiring, the second brother approached, and was burnt also. When these two had been repelled by the burning gold, last of all the youngest brother advanced]; upon him the gold had no effect, and he carried it to his house. The two elder brothers, observing what had happened, resigned all authority to the youngest.

6. From Lipoxais those Scythians were descended who are termed the Auchatæ; from Arpoxais, the second brother, those who are called the Catiari and the Traspies; from the youngest, who was king, came the Paralatæ. Generally speaking, these people are named Scoloti, from a surname of their king, but the Greeks call them Scythians.

7. This is the account which the Scythians give of their origin; and they add that from their first king Targitaus to the invasion of their country by Darius, is a period of a thousand years, and no more. The sacred gold is preserved by their kings with the greatest care; and every year there are solemn sacrifices, at which the prince assists. They have a tradition that if the person who has the custody of this gold sleeps in the open air during the time of their annual festival, he dies before the end of the year; for this reason they give him as much land as he can pass over on horseback in the

course of a day. As this region is extensive, King Colaxais divided the country into three parts, which he gave to three sons, making that portion the largest in which the gold was deposited. As to the district which lies farther to the north, and beyond the extreme inhabitants of the country, they say that it neither can be passed, nor yet discerned with the eye, on account of the feathers which are continually falling. With these both the earth and the air are so filled as effectually to obstruct the view.

8. Such is the manner in which the Scythians describe themselves and the country beyond them. The Greeks who inhabit Pontus speak of both as follows: Hercules, when he was driving away the heifers of Geryon, came to this region, now inhabited by the Scythians, but which then was a desert. This Geryon lived beyond Pontus, in an island which the Greeks call Erythia, near Gades, which is situate in the ocean, and beyond the Columns of Hercules. The ocean, they say, commencing at the east, flows round all the earth; this, however, they affirm without proving it. Hercules, coming from thence, arrived at this country, now called Scythia, where, finding himself overtaken by a severe storm, and being exceedingly cold, he wrapped himself up in his lion's skin, and went to sleep. They add that his mares, which

he had detached from his chariot to feed, by some divine interposition, disappeared during his sleep.

9. As soon as he awoke, he wandered over all the country in search of his mares, till at length he came to the district which is called **Hylæa**; there in a cave he discovered a female of most unnatural appearance, resembling a woman as far as the thighs, but whose lower parts were like a serpent. Hercules beheld her with astonishment, but he was not deterred from asking her whether she had seen his mares? She made answer that they were in her custody; she refused, however, to restore them, but upon condition of his dwelling with her. The terms proposed induced Hercules to consent; but she still deferred restoring his mares, from the wish of retaining him longer with her, whilst Hercules was equally anxious to obtain them and depart. After awhile she restored them with these words:—" Your mares, which wandered here, I have preserved; you have paid what was due to my care. I have conceived by you three sons; I wish you to say how I shall dispose of them hereafter; whether I shall detain them here, where I am the sole sovereign, or whether I shall send them to you." The reply of Hercules was to this effect:—" As soon as they shall be grown up to man's estate, observe this, and you cannot err; whichever of them you shall see bend this bow,

and wear this belt as I do, him detain in this country; the others, who shall not be able to do this, you may send away. By minding what I say you will have pleasure yourself, and will satisfy my wishes."

10. Having said this, Hercules took one of his bows, for thus far he had carried two, and showing her also his belt, at the end of which a golden cup was suspended, he gave her them, and departed. As soon as the boys of whom she was delivered grew up, she called the eldest Agathyrsus, the second Gelonus, and the youngest Scytha. She remembered also the injunctions she had received; and two of her sons, Agathyrsus and Gelonus, who were incompetent to the trial which was proposed, were sent away by their mother from this country. Scytha the youngest was successful in his exertions, and remained. From this Scytha, the son of Hercules, the Scythian monarchs are descended; and from the golden cup the Scythians to this day have a cup at the end of their belts.

11. This is the story which the Greek inhabitants of Pontus relate; but there is also another, to which I am more inclined to assent:—The Scythian nomades of Asia, having been harassed by the Massagetæ in war, passed the Araxis, and settled in Cimmeria; for it is to be observed that the country now possessed by the Scythians belonged

formerly to the Cimmerians. This people, when attacked by the Scythians, deliberated what it was most advisable to do against the inroad of so vast a multitude. Their sentiments were divided; both were violent, but that of the kings appears preferable. The people were of opinion that it would be better not to hazard an engagement, but to retreat in security; the kings were at all events for resisting the enemy. Neither party would recede from their opinions, the people and the princes mutually refusing to yield; the people wished to retire before the invaders; the princes determined rather to die where they were, reflecting upon what they had enjoyed before, and alarmed by the fears of future calamities. From verbal disputes they soon came to actual engagement, and they happened to be nearly equal in number. All those who perished by the hands of their countrymen were buried by the Cimmerians near the river Tyré, where their monuments may still be seen. The survivors fled from their country, which in its abandoned state was seized and occupied by the Scythians.

12. There are still to be found in Scythia walls and bridges which are termed Cimmerian; the same name is also given to a whole district, as well as to a narrow sea. It is certain that when the Cimmerians were expelled their country by the

Scythians, they fled to the Asiatic Chersonese, where the Greek city of Sinopé is at present situated. It is also apparent that, whilst engaged in the pursuit, the Scythians deviated from their proper course, and entered Media. The Cimmerians in their flight kept uniformly by the sea-coast; but the Scythians, having Mount Caucasus to their right, continued the pursuit till, by following an inland direction, they entered Media.

13. There is still another account, which has obtained credit both with the Greeks and barbarians. Aristeas, the poet, a native of Proconnesus, and son of Caustrobius, relates that under the influence of Apollo he came to the Issedones; that beyond this people he found the Arimaspi, a nation who have but one eye; farther on were the Gryphins, the guardians of the gold; and beyond these the Hyperboreans, who possess the whole country quite to the sea; and that all these nations, except the Hyperboreans, are continually engaged in war with their neighbours. Of these hostilities the Arimaspians were the first authors, for they drove out the Issedones, who did the same to the Scythians; the Scythians compelled the Cimmerians, who possessed the country towards the south, to abandon their native land. Thus it appears that the narrative of Aristeas differs also from that of the Scythians.

14. Of what country the relater of the above account was we have already seen; but I ought not to omit what I have heard of this personage, both at Proconnesus and Cyzicus. It is said of this Aristeas that he was of one of the best families of his country, and that he died in the workshop of a fuller, into which he had accidentally gone. The fuller immediately secured his shop, and went to inform the relations of the deceased of what had happened. The report having circulated through the city that Aristeas was dead, there came a man of Cyzicus, of the city of Artaces, who affirmed that this assertion was false, for that he had met Aristeas going to Cyzicus, and had spoken with him. In consequence of his positive assertions, the friends of Aristeas hastened to the fuller's shop with everything which was necessary for his funeral, but, when they came there, no Aristeas was to be found, alive or dead. Seven years afterwards, it is said that he re-appeared at Proconnesus, and composed those verses which the Greeks call Arimaspian, after which he vanished a second time.

15. This is the manner in which these cities speak of Aristeas. But I am about to relate a circumstance which, to my own knowledge, happened to the Metapontines of Italy, three hundred and forty years after Aristeas had a second time disappeared, according to my conjecture, as it

agrees with what I heard at Proconnesus and Metapontus. The inhabitants of this latter place affirm that Aristeas, having appeared in their city, directed them to construct an altar to Apollo, and near it a statue to Aristeas of Proconnesus. He told them that they were the only people of Italy whom Apollo had ever honoured by his presence, and that he himself had attended the god under the form of a crow; having said this, he disappeared. The Metapontines relate that, in consequence of this, they sent to Delphi to inquire what that unnatural appearance might mean. The Pythian told them, in reply, to perform what had been directed, for that they would find their obedience rewarded. They obeyed accordingly, and there now stands near the statue of Apollo himself another bearing the name of Aristeas; it is placed in the public square of the city, surrounded with laurels.

16. Thus much of Aristeas. No certain knowledge is to be obtained of the places which lie remotely beyond the country of which I before spake. On this subject I could not meet with any person able to speak from his own knowledge. Aristeas above-mentioned confesses, in the poem which he wrote, that he did not penetrate beyond the Issedones; and that what he related of the countries more remote, he learned of the Issedones themselves. For my own part, all the intelligence

which the most assiduous researches and the greatest attention to authenticity, have been able to procure, shall be faithfully related.

17. As we advance from the port of the Borysthenites, which is unquestionably the centre of all the maritime parts of Scythia, the first people who are met with are the Callipidæ, who are Greek Scythians: beyond these is another nation, called the Halizones. These two people in general observe the customs of the Scythians, except that for food they sow corn, onions, garlick, lentils, and millet. Beyond the Halizones dwell some Scythian husbandmen, who sow corn not to eat, but for sale. Still more remote are the Neuri, whose country towards the north, as far as I have been able to learn, is totally uninhabited. All these nations dwell near the river Hypanis, to the west of the Borysthenes.

18. Having crossed the Borysthenes, the first country towards the sea is Hylæa, contiguous to which are some Scythian husbandmen, who call themselves Olbiopolitæ, but who, by the Greeks living near the Hypanis, are called Borysthenites. The country possessed by these Scythians towards the east is the space of a three days' journey, as far as the river Panticapes; to the north, their lands extend to the amount of an eleven days' voyage along the Borysthenes. The space beyond

this is a vast inhospitable desert; and remoter still are the Androphagi, or men-eaters, a separate nation and by no means Scythian. As we pass farther from these, the country is altogether desert, not containing, to our knowledge, any inhabitants.

19. To the east of these Scythians, who are husbandmen, and beyond the river Panticapes, are the Scythian nomades or shepherds, who are totally unacquainted with agriculture; except Hylæa, all this country is naked of trees. These nomades inhabit a district to the extent of a fourteen days' journey towards the east, as far as the river Gerrhus.

20. Beyond the Gerrhus is situate what is termed the royal province of Scythia, possessed by the more numerous part and the noblest of the Scythians, who consider all the rest of their countrymen as their slaves. From the south they extend to Tauris, and from the east as far as the trench which was sunk by the descendants of the blinded slaves, and again as far as the port of the Palus Mæotis, called Chemni; and indeed many of them are spread as far as the Tanaïs. Beyond these, to the north, live the Melanchlæni, another nation who are not Scythians. Beyond the Melanchlæni, the lands are low and marshy, and as we believe entirely uninhabited.

21. Beyond the Tanaïs the region of Scythia

terminates, and the first nation we meet with are the Sauromatæ, who, commencing at the remote parts of the Palus Mæotis, inhabit a space to the north equal to a fifteen days' journey; the country is totally destitute of trees, both wild and cultivated. Beyond these are the Budini, who are husbandmen, and in whose country trees are found in great abundance.

22. To the north, beyond the Budini, is an immense desert of eight days' journey; passing which to the east are the Thyssagetæ, a singular but populous nation, who support themselves by hunting. Contiguous to these, in the same region, are a people called Iyrcæ; they also live by the chase, which they thus pursue:—Having ascended the tops of the trees, which everywhere abound, they watch for their prey. Each man has a horse, instructed to lie close to the ground, that it may not be seen; they have each also a dog. As soon as the man from the tree discovers his game, he wounds it with an arrow, then mounting his horse he pursues it, followed by his dog. Advancing from this people still nearer to the east, we again meet with Scythians, who having seceded from the royal Scythians, established themselves here.

23. As far as these Scythians, the whole country is flat, and the soil excellent; beyond them it becomes barren and stony. After travelling over a

considerable space, a people are found living at the foot of some lofty mountains, who, both male and female, are said to be bald from their birth, having large chins, and nostrils like the ape species. They have a language of their own, but their dress is Scythian; they live chiefly upon the produce of a tree which is called the ponticus; it is as large as a fig, and has a kernel not unlike a bean: when it is ripe they press it through a cloth; it produces a thick black liquor which they call aschy: this they drink, mixing it with milk; the grosser parts which remain they form into balls and eat. They have but few cattle, from the want of proper pasturage. Each man dwells under his tree; this during the winter they cover with a thick white cloth, which in the summer is removed; they live unmolested by any one, being considered as sacred, and having among them no offensive weapon. Their neighbours apply to them for decision in matters of private controversy; and whoever seeks an asylum amongst them is secure from injury. They are called the Argippæi.

24. As far as these people who are bald, the knowledge of the country and intermediate nations is clear and satisfactory; it may be obtained from the Scythians, who have frequent communication with them, from the Greeks of the port on the Borysthenes, and from many other places of trade

on the Euxine. As these nations have seven different languages, the Scythians who communicate with them have occasion for as many interpreters.

25. Beyond these Argippæi, no certain intelligence is to be had, a chain of lofty and inaccessible mountains precluding all discovery. The people who are bald assert, what I can by no means believe, that these mountains are inhabited by men, who in their lower parts resemble a goat; and that beyond these are a race who sleep away six months of the year: neither does this seem at all more probable. To the east of the Argippæi it is beyond all doubt that the country is possessed by the Issedones; but beyond them to the north neither the Issedones nor the Argippæi know anything more than I have already related.

26. The Issedones have these, among other customs:—As often as any one loses his father, his relations severally provide some cattle; these they kill, and having cut them in pieces, they dismember also the body of the deceased, and, mixing the whole together, feast upon it; the head alone is preserved; from this they carefully remove the hair, and, cleansing it thoroughly, set it in gold: it is afterwards esteemed sacred, and produced in their solemn annual sacrifices. Every man observes the above rites in honour of his father, as the

Greeks do theirs in memory of the dead. In other respects it is said that they venerate the principles of justice; and that their females enjoy equal authority with the men.

27. The Issedones themselves affirm that the country beyond them is inhabited by a race of men who have but one eye, and by Gryphins who are guardians of the gold. Such is the information which the Scythians have from the Issedones, and we from the Scythians; in the Scythian tongue they are called Arimaspians, from Arima, the Scythian word for one, and spu, an eye.

28. Through all the reigon of which we have been speaking, the winter season, which continues for eight months, is intolerably severe and cold. At this time, if water be poured upon the ground, unless it be near a fire, it will not make clay. The sea itself, and all the Cimmerian Bosphorus, is congealed; and the Scythians, who live within the trench before mentioned, make hostile incursions upon the ice, and penetrate with their waggons as far as Sindica. During eight months the climate is thus severe, and the remaining four are sufficiently cold. In this region the winter is by no means the same as in other climates; for at this time, when it rains abundantly elsewhere, it here scarcely rains at all, whilst in the summer the rains are incessant. At the season when thunder is

common in other places, here it is never heard, but during the summer it is very heavy. If it be ever known to thunder in winter, it is considered as ominous. If earthquakes happen in Scythia in either season of the year, it is thought a prodigy. Their horses are able to bear the extremest severity of the climate, which the asses and mules frequently cannot; though in other reigons the cold which destroys the former has little effect upon the latter.

29. This circumstance of their climate seems to explain the reason why their cattle are without horns; and Homer in the "Odyssey" has a line which confirms my opinion:—"And Libya where the sheep have always horns," which is as much as to say that in warm climates horns will readily grow; but in places which are extremely cold they either will not grow at all, or are always diminutive.

30. The peculiarities of Scythia are thus explained from the coldness of the climate; but as I have accustomed myself from the commencement of this history to deviate occasionally from my subject, I cannot here avoid expressing my surprise that the district of Elis never produces mules; yet the air is by no means cold, nor can any other satisfactory reason be assigned. The inhabitants themselves believe that their not possessing mules is the effect

of some curse. When their mares require the male, the Eleans take them out of the limits of their own territories, and there suffer asses to cover them; when they have conceived they return.

31. Concerning those feathers, which, as the Scythians say, so cloud the atmosphere that they cannot penetrate nor even discern what lies beyond them, my opinion is this:—In those remoter regions there is a perpetual fall of snow, which, as may be supposed, is less in summer than in winter. Whoever observes snow falling continually will easily conceive what I say; for it has a great resemblance to feathers. These regions, therefore, which are thus situated remotely to the north, are uninhabitable from the unremitting severity of the climate; and the Scythians, with the neighbouring nations, mistake the snow for feathers. But on this subject I have said quite enough.

32. Of the Hyperboreans neither the Scythians nor any of the neighbouring people, the Issedones alone excepted, have any knowledge; and indeed what they say merits but little attention. The Scythians speak of these as they do of the Arimaspians. It must be confessed that "Hesiod" mentions these Hyperboreans, as Homer also does in the "Epigonoi," if he was really the author of those verses.

33. On this subject of the Hyperboreans, the

Delians are more communicative. They affirm that some sacred offerings of this people, carefully folded in straw, were given to the Scythians, from whom descending regularly through every contiguous nation, they arrived at length at the Adriatic. From hence, transported towards the south, they were first of all received by the Dodoneans of Greece; from them again they were transmitted to the Gulf of Melis; whence, passing into Euboea, they were sent from one town to another, till they arrived at Carystus; not stopping at Andros, the Carystians carried them to Tenos, the Tenians to Delos: at which place the Delians affirm they came as we have related. They farther observe, that to bring these offerings the Hyperboreans sent two young women, whose names were Hyperoche and Laodice: five of their countrymen accompanied them as a guard, who are held in great veneration at Delos, and called the Peripheres. As these men never returned the Hyperboreans were greatly offended, and took the following method to prevent a repetition of this evil:— They carried to their frontiers their offerings, folded in barley-straw, and committing them to the care of their neighbours, directed them to forward them progressively, till, as is reported, they thus arrived at Delos. This singularity observed by the Hyperboreans is practised, as I myself have seen, amongst the women of Thrace and Pæonia, who in their sacrifices to the regal Diana make use of barley-straw.

34. In honour of the Hyperborean virgins who died at Delos, the Delian youth of both sexes celebrate certain rites, in which they cut off their hair; this ceremony is observed by virgins previous to their marriage, who, having deprived themselves of their hair, wind it round a spindle, and place it on the tomb. This stands in the vestibule of the temple of Diana, on the left side of the entrance, and is shaded by an olive, which grows there naturally. The young men of Delos wind some of their hair round a certain herb, and place it on the tomb. Such are the honours which the Delians pay to these virgins.

35. The Delians add that, in the same age, and before the arrival of Hyperoche and Laodice at Delos, two other Hyperborean virgins came there, whose names were Argis and Opis; their object was to bring an offering to Lucina, in acknowledgment of the happy delivery of their females; but that Argis and Opis were accompanied by the deities themselves. They are, therefore, honoured with other solemn rites. The women assemble together, and in a hymn composed for the occasion by Olen of Lycia, they call on the names of Argis and Opis. Instructed by these, the islanders and

Ionians hold similar assemblies, introducing the same two names in their hymns. This Olen was a native of Lycia, who composed other ancient hymns in use at Delos. When the thighs of the victims are consumed on the altar, the ashes are collected and scattered over the tomb of Opis and Argis. This tomb is behind the temple of Diana, facing the east, and near the place where the Ceians celebrate their festivals.

36. Concerning these Hyperboreans we have spoken sufficiently at large, for the story of Abaris, who was said to be a Hyperborean, and to have made a circuit of the earth without food, and carried on an arrow, merits no attention. As there are Hyperboreans, or inhabitants of the extreme parts of the north, one would suppose there ought also to be Hypernotians, or inhabitants of the corresponding parts of the south. For my own part, I cannot but think it exceedingly ridiculous to hear some men talk of the circumference of the earth, pretending, without the smallest reason or probability, that the ocean encompasses the earth; that the earth is round, as if mechanically formed so; and that Asia is equal to Europe. I will, therefore, concisely describe the figure and the size of each of these portions of the earth.

37. The region occupied by the Persians extends southward to the Red Sea; beyond these to the

north are the Medes, next to them are the Sapirians. Contiguous to the Sapirians, and where the Phasis empties itself into the Northern Sea, are the Colchians. These four nations occupy the space between the two seas.

38. From hence to the west, two tracts of land stretch themselves towards the sea, which I shall describe: The one on the north side commences at the Phasis, and extends to the sea along the Euxine and the Hellespont, as far as the Sigeum of Troy. On the south side it begins at the bay of Margandius, contiguous to Phœnicia, and is continued to the sea as far as the Triopian promontory; this space of country is inhabited by thirty different nations.

39. The other district commences in Persia, and is continued to the Red Sea. Besides Persia, it comprehends Assyria and Arabia, naturally terminating in the Arabian Gulf, into which Darius introduced a channel of the Nile. The interval from Persia to Phœnicia is very extensive. From Phœnicia it again continues beyond Syria of Palestine, as far as Egypt, where it terminates. The whole of this region is occupied by three nations only. Such is the division of Asia from Persia westward.

40. To the east beyond Persia, Media, the Sapirians, and Colchians, the country is bounded

by the Red Sea; to the north by the Caspian and the river Araxes, which directs its course towards the east. As far as India, Asia is well inhabited; but from India eastward the whole country is one vast desert, unknown and unexplored.

41. The second tract comprehends Libya, which begins where Egypt ends. About Egypt the country is very narrow. One hundred thousand orgyiæ, or one thousand stadia, comprehend the space between this and the Red Sea. Here the country expands, and takes the name of Libya.

42. I am much surprised at those who have divided and defined the limits of Libya, Asia, and Europe, betwixt which the difference is far from small. Europe, for instance, in length much exceeds the other two, but is of far inferior breadth. Except in that particular part which is contiguous to Asia, the whole of Libya is surrounded by the sea. The first person who has proved this was, as far as we are able to judge, Necho, King of Egypt. When he had desisted from his attempt to join by a canal the Nile with the Arabian Gulf, he despatched some vessels, under the conduct of Phœnicians, with directions to pass by the columns of Hercules, and after penetrating the Northern Ocean to return to Egypt. These Phœnicians, taking their course from the Red Sea, entered into

the Southern Ocean. On the approach of autumn they landed in Libya, and planted some corn in the place where they happened to find themselves; when this was ripe, and they had cut it down, they again departed. Having thus consumed two years, they in the third doubled the columns of Hercules, and returned to Egypt. Their relation may obtain attention from others, but to me it seems incredible, for they affirmed that, having sailed round Libya, they had the sun on their right hand. Thus was Libya for the first time known.

43. If the Carthaginian account may be credited, Sataspes, son of Teaspes, of the race of the Achæmenides, received a commission to circumnavigate Libya, which he never executed. Alarmed by the length of the voyage, and the solitary appearance of the country, he returned without accomplishing the task enjoined him by his mother. This man had committed violence on a virgin, daughter of Zopyrus, son of Megabyzus, for which offence Xerxes had ordered him to be crucified; but the influence of his mother, who was sister to Darius, saved his life. She avowed, however, that it was her intention to inflict a still severer punishment upon him, by obliging him to sail round Libya, till he should arrive at the Arabian Gulf. To this Xerxes assented, and Sataspes accordingly departed

for Egypt; he here embarked with his crew, and proceeded to the columns of Hercules; passing these, he doubled the promontory which is called Syloes, keeping a southern course. Continuing his voyage for several months, in which he passed over an immense tract of sea, he saw no probable termination of his labours, and therefore sailed back to Egypt. Returning to the court of Xerxes, he amongst other things related that, in the most remote places he had visited, he had seen a people of diminutive appearance, clothed in red garments, who on the approach of his vessel to the shore, had deserted their habitations, and fled to the mountains. But he affirmed that his people, satisfied with taking a supply of provisions, offered them no violence. He denied the possibility of his making the circuit of Libya, as his vessel was totally unable to proceed. Xerxes gave no credit to his assertions; and, as he had not fulfilled the terms imposed upon him, he was executed according to his former sentence. A eunuch belonging to this Sataspes, hearing of his master's death, fled with a great sum of money to Samos, but he was there robbed of his property by a native of the place, whose name I know but forbear to mention.

44. A very considerable part of Asia was first discovered by Darius. He was extremely desirous of ascertaining where the Indus meets the ocean,

the only river but one in which crocodiles are found. To effect this, he sent, among other men in whom he could confide, Scylax of Caryandia. Departing from Caspatyrus in the Pactyian territories, they followed the eastern course of the river, till they came to the sea; then sailing westward, they arrived, after a voyage of thirty months, at the very point from whence, as I have before related, the Egyptian prince despatched the Phœnicians to circumnavigate Libya. After this voyage, Darius subdued the Indians, and became master of that ocean; whence it appears that Asia in all its parts, except those more remotely to the east, entirely resembles Libya.

45. It is certain that Europe has not hitherto been carefully examined; it is by no means determined whether to the east and north it is limited by the ocean. In length it unquestionably exceeds the two other divisions of the earth; but I am far from satisfied why to one continent three different names, taken from women, have been assigned. To one of these divisions some have given as a boundary the Egyptian Nile, and the Colchian Phasis; others the Tanaïs, the Cimmerian Bosphorus, and the Palus Mæotis. The names of those who have thus distinguished the earth, or the first occasion of their different appellations, I have never been able to learn. Libya is by many

of the Greeks said to have been so named from Libya, a woman of the country; and Asia from the wife of Prometheus. The Lydians contradict this, and affirm that Asia was so called from Asias, a son of Cotys, and grandson of Manis, and not from the wife of Prometheus; to confirm this, they adduce the name of a tribe at Sardis, called the Asian tribe. It has certainly never been ascertained whether Europe be surrounded by the ocean: it is a matter of equal uncertainty whence or from whom it derives its name. We cannot willingly allow that it took its name from the Syrian Europa, though we know that, like the other two, it was formerly without any. We are well assured that Europa was an Asiatic, and that she never saw the region which the Greeks now call Europe; she only went from Phœnicia to Crete; from Crete to Lycia. I shall now quit this subject, upon which I have given the opinions generally received.

46. Except Scythia, the countries of the Euxine, against which Darius undertook an expedition, are of all others the most barbarous; among the people who dwell within these limits, we have found no individual of superior learning and accomplishments but Anacharsis the Scythian. Even of the Scythian nation I cannot in general speak with extraordinary commendation; they have,

however, one observance, which for its wisdom excels everything I have met with. The possibility of escape is cut off from those who attack them; and if they are averse to be seen, their places of retreat can never be discovered: for they have no towns nor fortified cities; their habitations they constantly carry along with them; their bows and arrows they manage on horseback; and they support themselves not by agriculture, but by their cattle; their constant abode may be said to be in their waggons. How can a people so circumstanced afford the means of victory, or even of attack?

47. Their particular mode of life may be imputed partly to the situation of their country, and the advantage they derive from their rivers; their lands are well watered, and well adapted for pasturage. The number of rivers is almost equal to the channels of the Nile; the more celebrated of them, and those which are navigable to the sea, I shall enumerate; they are these: the Danube, having five mouths; the Tyres, the Hypanis, the Borysthenes, Panticapes, Hypacyris, Gerrhus, and the Tanaïs.

48. No river of which we have any knowledge is so vast as the Danube; it is always of the same depth, experiencing no variation from summer or from winter. It is the first river of Scythia to the

east, and it is the greatest of all, for it is swelled by the influx of many others: there are five which particularly contribute to increase its size; one of these the Greeks call Pyreton, the Scythians, Porata; the other four are the Tiarantus, Ararus, Naparis, and the Ordessus. The first of these rivers is of immense size; flowing towards the east it mixes with the Danube: the second, the Tiarantus, is smaller, having an inclination to the west; betwixt these, the Ararus, Naparis, and Ordessus have their course, and empty themselves into the Danube. These rivers have their rise in Scythia, and swell the waters of the Danube.

49. The Maris also, commencing among the Agathyrsi, is emptied into the Danube, which is likewise the case with the three great rivers, Atlas, Auras, and Tibisis; these flow from the summits of Mount Hæmus, and have the same termination. Into the same river are received the waters of the Athres, Noes, and Artanes, which flow through Thrace, and the country of the Thracian Crobyzi. The Cius, which, rising in Pæonia, near Mount Rhodope, divides Mount Hæmus, is also poured into the Danube. The Angrus comes from Illyria, and with a northward course passes over the Tribalian plains, and mixes with the Brongus; the Brongus meets the Danube, which thus receives the waters of these two great rivers. The Carpis,

moreover, which rises in the country beyond the Umbrici, and the Alpis, which flows towards the north, are both lost in the Danube. Commencing with the Celtæ, who, except the Cynetæ, are the most remote inhabitants in the west of Europe, this river passes directly through the centre of Europe, and by a certain inclination enters Scythia.

50. By the union of these and of many other waters, the Danube becomes the greatest of all rivers; but if one be compared with another, the preference must be given to the Nile, into which no stream nor fountain enters. The reason why in the two opposite seasons of the year the Danube is uniformly the same, seems to me to be this: in the winter it is at its full natural height, or, perhaps, somewhat more, at which season there is, in the regions through which it passes, abundance of snow, but very little rain; but in the summer all this snow is dissolved, and emptied into the Danube, which, together with frequent and heavy rains, greatly augment it. But in proportion as the body of its waters is thus multiplied, are the exhalations of the summer sun. The result of this action and re-action on the Danube is that its waters are constantly of the same depth.

51. Thus, of the rivers which flow through Scythia, the Danube is the first; next to this is

the Tyres, which, rising in the north from an immense marsh, divides Scythia from Neuris. At the mouth of this river those Greeks live who are known by the name of the Tyritæ.

52. The third is the Hypanis; this comes from Scythia, rising from an immense lake, round which are found wild white horses, and which is properly enough called the mother of the Hypanis. This river, through a space of five days' journey from its first rise, is small, and its waters are sweet, but from thence to the sea, which is a journey of four days more, it becomes exceedingly bitter. This is occasioned by a small fountain, which it receives in its passage, and which is of so very bitter a quality, that it infects this river, though by no means contemptible in point of size: this fountain rises in the country of the ploughing Scythians, and of the Alazones. It takes the name of the place where it springs, which in the Scythian tongue is Exampæus, corresponding in Greek to the "Sacred Ways." In the district of the Alazones, the streams of the Tyres and the Hypanis have an inclination towards each other, but they soon separate again to a considerable distance.

53. The fourth river, and the largest next to the Danube, is the Borysthenes. In my opinion this river is more fertile, not only than all the rivers of

Scythia, but than every other in the world, except the Egyptian Nile. The Nile, it must be confessed, disdains all comparison; the Borysthenes nevertheless affords most agreeable and excellent pasturage, and contains great abundance of the more delicate fish. Although it flows in the midst of many turbid rivers, its waters are perfectly clear and sweet; its banks are adorned by the richest harvests, and in those places where corn is not sown the grass grows to a surprising height; at its mouth a large mass of salt is formed of itself. It produces also a species of large fish, which is called Antacæus; these, which have no prickly fins, the inhabitants salt. It possesses various other things which deserve our admiration. The course of the stream may be pursued as far as the country called Gerrhus through a voyage of forty days, and it is known to flow from the north. But of the remoter places through which it passes, no one can speak with certainty; it seems probable that it runs towards the district of the Scythian husbandmen through a pathless desert. For the space of a ten days' journey these Scythians inhabit its banks. The sources of this river, like those of the Nile, are to me unknown, as I believe they are to every other Greek. This river, as it approaches the sea, is joined by the Hypanis, and they have both the same termination. The neck of land betwixt these two streams is called the Hippoleon promontory, in which a temple is erected to Ceres. Beyond this temple, as far as the Hypanis, dwell the Borysthenites. But on this subject enough has been said.

54. Next to the above is a fifth river, called the Panticapes; this also rises in the north, and from a lake. The interval betwixt this and the Borysthenes is possessed by the Scythian husbandmen. Having passed through Hylæa, the Panticapes mixes with the Borysthenes.

55. The sixth river is called the Hypacyris; this, rising from a lake, and passing through the midst of the Scythian Nomades, empties itself into the sea near the town of Carcinitis. In its course it bounds to the right Hylæ, and what is called the course of Achilles.

56. The name of the seventh river is the Gerrhus; it takes its name from the place Gerrhus near which it separates itself from the Borysthenes, and where this latter river is first known. In its passage toward the sea it divides the Scythian Nomades from the Royal Scythians, and then mixes with the Hypacyris.

57. The eighth river is called the Tanaïs; rising from one immense lake, it empties itself into another still greater, named the Mæotis, which separates the Royal Scythians from the Sauro-

matæ. The Tanaïs is increased by the waters of another river, called the Hyrgis.

58. Thus the Scythians have the advantage of all these celebrated rivers. The grass which this country produces is of all that we know the fullest of moisture, which evidently appears from the dissection of their cattle.

59. We have shown that this people possess the greatest abundance; their particular laws and observances are these: Of their divinities, Vesta is without competition the first, then Jupiter and Tellus, whom they believe to be the wife of Jupiter; next to these are Apollo, the Celestial Venus, Hercules, and Mars. All the Scythians revere these as deities, but the Royal Scythians pay divine rites also to Neptune. In the Scythian tongue Vesta is called Tabiti; Jupiter, and as I think very properly, Papæus; Tellus, Apia; Apollo, Œtosyrus; the Celestial Venus, Artimpasa; and Neptune, Thamimasadas. Among all these deities, Mars is the only one to whom they think it proper to erect altars, shrines, and temples.

60. Their mode of sacrifice in every place appointed for the purpose is precisely the same, and it is this: The victim is secured with a rope by its two fore feet; the person who offers the sacrifice, standing behind, throws the animal down by means of this rope; as it falls he invokes the name of the

divinity to whom the sacrifice is offered; he then fastens a cord round the neck of the victim, and strangles it, by winding the cord round a stick; all this is done without fire, without libations, or without any of the ceremonies in use amongst us. When the beast is strangled, the sacrificer takes off its skin, and prepares to dress it.

61. As Scythia is very barren of wood, they have the following contrivance to dress the flesh of the victim:—Having flayed the animal, they strip the flesh from the bones, and if they have them at hand, they throw it into certain pots made in Scythia, and resembling the Lesbian caldrons, though somewhat larger; under these a fire is made with the bones. If these pots cannot be procured, they enclose the flesh with a certain quantity of water in the paunch of the victim, and make a fire with the bones as before. The bones being very inflammable, and the paunch without difficulty made to contain the flesh separated from the bone, the ox is thus made to dress itself, which is also the case with the other victims. When the whole is ready, he who sacrifices throws down with some solemnity before him the entrails, and the more choice pieces. They sacrifice different animals, but horses in particular.

62. Such are the sacrifices and ceremonies observed with respect to their other deities; but to

the god Mars the particular rites which are paid are these:— In every district they construct a temple to this divinity, of this kind; bundles of small wood are heaped together to the length of three stadia, and quite as broad, but not so high. The top is a regular square; three of the sides are steep and broken, but the fourth is an inclined plane, forming the ascent. To this place are every year brought one hundred and fifty waggons full of these bundles of wood to repair the structure, which the severity of the climate is apt to destroy. Upon the summit of such a pile each Scythian tribe places an ancient scimitar, which is considered as the shrine of Mars, and is annually honoured by the sacrifice of sheep and horses; indeed, more victims are offered to this deity than to all the other divinities. It is their custom also to sacrifice every hundredth captive, but in a different manner from their other victims. Having poured libations upon their heads, they cut their throats into a vessel placed for that purpose. With this, carried to the summit of the pile, they besmear the above-mentioned scimitar. Whilst this is doing above, the following ceremony is observed below: From these human victims they cut off the right arms close to the shoulder, and throw them up into the air. The ceremony being performed on each victim severally, they depart;

the arms remain where they happen to fall, the bodies elsewhere.

63. The above is a description of their sacrifices. Swine are never used for this purpose, nor will they suffer them to be kept in their country.

64. Their military customs are these:—Every Scythian drinks the blood of the first person he slays; the heads of all the enemies who fall by his hand in battle he presents to his king. This offering entitles him to a share of the plunder, which he could not otherwise claim. Their mode of stripping the skin from the head is this:—They make a circular incision behind the ears, then, taking hold of the head at the top, they gradually flay it, drawing it towards them. They next soften it in their hands, removing every fleshy part which may remain, by rubbing it with an ox's hide; they afterwards suspend it, thus prepared, from the bridles of their horses, when they both use it as a napkin, and are proud of it as a trophy. Whoever possesses the greater number of these is deemed the most illustrious. Some there are who sew together several of these portions of human skin, and convert them into a kind of shepherd's garment. There are others who preserve the skins of the right arms, nails and all, of such enemies as they kill, and use them as a covering for their quivers. The human skin is of all others certainly the

whitest, and of a very firm texture; many Scythians will take the whole skin of a man, and having stretched it upon wood, use it as a covering to their horses.

65. Such are the customs of this people. This treatment, however, of their enemies' heads, is not universal, it is only perpetrated on those whom they most detest. They cut off the skull, below the eyebrows, and having cleansed it thoroughly, if they are poor they merely cover it with a piece of leather; if they are rich, in addition to this, they decorate the inside with gold; it is afterwards used as a drinking cup. They do the same with respect to their nearest connections, if any dissensions have arisen, and they overcome them in combat before the king. If any stranger whom they deem of consequence happen to visit them, they make a display of these heads, and relate every circumstance of the previous connection, the provocations received, and their subsequent victory. This they consider as a testimony of their valour.

66. Once a year the prince or ruler of every district mixes a goblet of wine, of which those Scythians drink who have destroyed a public enemy. But of this, they who have not done such a thing are not permitted to taste; these are obliged to sit apart by themselves, which is considered as a mark of the greatest ignominy. They

who have killed a number of enemies are permitted on this occasion to drink from two cups joined together.

67. They have amongst them a great number who practise the art of divination; for this purpose they use a number of willow twigs in this manner:— They bring large bundles of these together, and having untied them, dispose them one by one on the ground, each bundle at a distance from the rest. This done, they pretend to foretell the future, during which they take up the bundles separately, and tie them again together. This mode of divination is hereditary among them. The enaries, or "effeminate men," affirm that the art of divination was taught them by the goddess Venus. They take also the leaves of the lime-tree, which dividing into three parts they twine round their fingers; they then unbind it, and exercise the art to which they pretend.

68. Whenever the Scythian monarch happens to be indisposed, he sends for three of the most celebrated of these diviners. When the Scythians desire to use the most solemn kind of oath, they swear by the king's throne. These diviners, therefore, make no scruple of affirming that such or such individual, pointing him out by name, has forsworn himself by the royal throne. Immediately the person thus marked out is seized, and informed

that by their art of divination, which is infallible, he has been indirectly the occasion of the king's illness, by having violated the oath which we have mentioned. If the accused not only denies the charge, but expresses himself enraged at the imputation, the king convokes a double number of diviners, who, examining into the mode which has been pursued in criminating him, decide accordingly. If he be found guilty, he immediately loses his head, and the three diviners who were first consulted share his effects. If these last diviners acquit the accused, others are at hand, of whom, if the greater number absolve him, the first diviners are put to death.

69. The manner in which they are executed is this:—Some oxen are yoked to a waggon filled with fagots, in the midst of which, with their feet tied, their hands fastened behind, and their mouths gagged, these diviners are placed; fire is then set to the wood, and the oxen are terrified, to make them run violently away. It sometimes happens that the oxen themselves are burned; and often, when the waggon is consumed, the oxen escape severely scorched. This is the method by which, for the above-mentioned or similar offences, they put to death those whom they call false diviners.

70. Of those whom the king condemns to death, he constantly destroys the male children, leaving

the females unmolested. Whenever the Scythians form alliances, they observe these ceremonies:—A large earthen vessel is filled with wine; into this is poured some of the blood of the contracting parties, obtained by a slight incision of a knife or a sword; in this cup they dip a scimitar, some arrows, a hatchet, and a spear. After this, they pronounce some solemn prayers, and the parties who form the contract, with such of their friends as are of superior dignity, finally drink the contents of the vessel.

71. The sepulchres of the kings are in the district of the Gerrhi. As soon as the king dies, a large trench of a quadrangular form is sunk, near where the Borysthenes begins to be navigable. When this has been done, the body is enclosed in wax, after it has been thoroughly cleansed, and the entrails taken out; before it is sewn up, they fill it with anise, parsley-seed, bruised cypress, and various aromatics. They then place it on a carriage, and remove it to another district, where the persons who receive it, like the Royal Scythians, cut off a part of their ear, shave their heads in a circular form, take a round piece of flesh from their arm, wound their foreheads and noses, and pierce their left hands with arrows. The body is again carried to another province of the deceased king's realms, the inhabitants of the

former district accompanying the procession. After thus transporting the dead body through the different provinces of the kingdom, they come at last to the Gerrhi, who live in the remotest parts of Scythia, and amongst whom the sepulchres are. Here the corpse is placed upon a couch, round which, at different distances, daggers are fixed; upon the whole are disposed pieces of wood, covered with branches of willow. In some other part of this trench they bury one of the deceased's concubines, whom they previously strangle, together with the baker, the cook, the groom, his most confidential servant, his horses, the choicest of his effects, and, finally, some golden goblets, for they possess neither silver nor brass: to conclude all, they fill up the trench with earth, and seem to be emulous in their endeavours to raise as high a mound as possible.

72. The ceremony does not terminate here. They select such of the deceased king's attendants, in the following year, as have been most about his person; these are all native Scythians, for in Scythia there are no purchased slaves, the king selecting such to attend him as he thinks proper: fifty of these they strangle, with an equal number of his best horses. They open and cleanse the bodies of them all, which, having filled with straw, they sew up again; then upon two pieces of wood

they place a third, of a semicircular form, with its concave side uppermost; a second is disposed in like manner, then a third, and so on, till a sufficient number have been erected. Upon these semicircular pieces of wood they place the horses, after passing large poles through them, from the feet to the neck. One part of the structure, formed as we have described, supports the shoulders of the horse, the other his hinder parts, whilst the legs are left to project upwards. The horses are then bridled, and the reins fastened to the legs; upon each of these they afterwards place one of the youths who have been strangled, in the following manner: a pole is passed through each, quite to the neck, through the back, the extremity of which is fixed to the piece of timber with which the horse has been spitted; having done this with each, they so leave them.

73. The above are the ceremonies observed in the interment of their kings: as to the people in general, when any one dies, the neighbours place the body on a carriage, and carry it about to the different acquaintance of the deceased; these prepare some entertainment for those who accompany the corpse, placing the same before the body, as before the rest. Private persons, after being thus carried about for the space of forty days, are then buried. They who have been engaged in the

performance of these rites, afterwards use the following mode of purgation:—After thoroughly washing the head, and then drying it, they do thus with regard to the body; they place in the ground three stakes, inclining towards each other; round these they bind fleeces of wool as thickly as possible, and finally, into the space betwixt the stakes they throw red-hot stones.

74. They have among them a species of hemp resembling flax, except that it is both thicker and larger; it is indeed superior to flax, whether it is cultivated or grows spontaneously. Of this the Thracians make themselves garments, which so nearly resemble those of flax as to require a skilful eye to distinguish them: they who had never seen this hemp, would conclude these vests to be made of flax.

75. The Scythians take the seed of this hemp, and placing it beneath the woollen fleeces which we have before described, they throw it upon the red-hot stones, when immediately a perfumed vapour ascends stronger than from any Grecian stove. This, to the Scythians, is in the place of a bath, and it excites from them cries of exultation. It is to be observed, that they never bathe themselves: the Scythian women bruise under a stone some wood of the cypress, cedar, and frankincense; upon this they pour a quantity of water, till it

becomes of a certain consistency, with which they anoint the body and the face; this at the time imparts an agreeable odour, and when removed on the following day, gives the skin a soft and beautiful appearance.

76. The Scythians have not only a great abhorrence of all foreign customs, but each province seems unalterably tenacious of its own. Those of the Greek they particularly avoid, as appears both from Anacharsis and Scyles. Of Anacharsis, it is remarkable that, having personally visited a large part of the habitable world, and acquired great wisdom, he at length returned to Scythia. In his passage over the Hellespont, he touched at Cyzicus at the time when the inhabitants were celebrating a solemn and magnificent festival to the mother of the gods. He made a vow, that if he should return safe and without injury to his country, he would institute, in honour of his deity, the same rites which he had seen performed at Cyzicus, together with the solemnities observed on the eve of her festival. Arriving therefore in Scythia, in the district of Hylæa, near the Course of Achilles, a place abounding with trees, he performed all the particulars of the above-mentioned ceremonies, having a number of small statues fastened about him, with a cymbal in his hand. In this situation he was observed by one of the natives, who gave

intelligence of what he had seen to Saulius, the Scythian king. The king went instantly to the place, and, seeing Anacharsis so employed, killed him with an arrow. If any inquiries are now made concerning this Anacharsis, the Scythians disclaim all knowledge of him, merely because he visited Greece, and had learned some foreign customs. But I have been informed by Timnes, the tutor of Spargapithes, that Anacharsis was the uncle of Idanthyrsus, a Scythian king, and that he was the son of Gnurus, grandson of Lycus, and great-grandson of Spargapithes. If, therefore, this genealogy be true, it appears that Anacharsis was killed by his own brother, for Saulius, who killed Anacharsis, was the father of Idanthyrsus.

77. It is proper to acknowledge that from the Peloponnesians I have received a very different account. They affirm that Anacharsis was sent by the Scythian monarch to Greece for the express purpose of improving himself in science ; and they add that, at his return, he informed his employer that all the people of Greece were occupied in scientific pursuits, except the Lacedæmonians ; but they alone endeavoured to perfect themselves in discreet and wise conversation. This, however, is a tale of Grecian invention. I am convinced that Anacharsis was killed in the manner which has been described, and that he owed his destruction

to the practice of foreign customs and Grecian manners.

78. Not many years afterwards Scyles, the son of Aripithes, experienced a similar fortune. Aripithes, king of Scythia, amongst many other children, had this son Scyles by a woman of Istria, who taught him the language and sciences of Greece. It happened that Aripithes was treasonably put to death by Spargapithes, king of the Agathyrsi. He was succeeded in his dominions by this Scyles, who married one of his father's wives, whose name was Opæa. Opæa was a native of Scythia, and had a son named Oricus by her former husband. When Scyles ascended the Scythian throne, he was exceedingly averse to the manners of his country, and very partial to those of Greece, to which he had been accustomed from his childhood. As often therefore as he conducted the Scythian forces to the city of the Borysthenites, who affirm that they are descended from the Milesians, he left his army before the town, and entering into the place, secured the gates. He then threw aside his Scythian dress, and assumed the habit of Greece. In this, without guards or attendants, it was his custom to parade through the public square, having the caution to place guards at the gates, that no one of his countrymen might discover him. He not only thus showed his partiality to the customs

of Greece, but he also sacrificed to the gods in the Grecian manner. After continuing in the city for the space of a month, and sometimes for more, he would resume his Scythian dress and depart. This he frequently repeated, having built a palace in this town, and married an inhabitant of the place.

79. It seemed, however, ordained that his end should be unfortunate, which accordingly happened. It was his desire to be initiated into the mysteries of Bacchus, and he was already about to take some of the sacred utensils in his hands, when the following prodigy appeared to him. I have before mentioned the palace which he had in the city of the Borysthenites; it was a very large and magnificent structure, and the front of it was decorated with sphinxes and griffins of white marble; the lightning of heaven descended upon it, and it was totally consumed. Scyles nevertheless persevered in what he had undertaken. The Scythians reproach the Greeks on account of their Bacchanalian festivals, and assert it to be contrary to reason to suppose that any deity should prompt men to acts of madness. When the initiation of Scyles was completed, one of the Borysthenites discovered to the Scythians what he had done. "You Scythians," says he, "censure us on account of our Bacchanalian rites, when we yield to the impulse of the deity. This same deity has taken possession

of your sovereign; he is now obedient in his service, and under the influence of his power. If you disbelieve my words, you have only to follow me, and have ocular proof that what I say is true." The principal Scythians accordingly followed him, and by a secret avenue were by him conducted to the citadel. When they beheld Scyles approaching with his thiasus, and in every other respect acting the Bacchanal, they deemed the matter of most calamitous importance, and returning, informed the army of all that they had seen.

80. As soon as Scyles returned, an insurrection was excited against him, and his brother Octomasades, whose mother was the daughter of Tereus, was promoted to the throne. Scyles having learned the particulars and the motives of this revolt, fled into Thrace, against which place, as soon as he was informed of this event, Octomasades advanced with an army. The Thracians met him at the Ister; when they were upon the point of engaging, Sitalces sent a herald to Octomasades, with this message: "A contest betwixt us would be absurd, for you are the son of my sister. My brother is in your power; if you will deliver him to me, I will give up Scyles to you; thus we shall mutually avoid all danger." As the brother of Sitalces had taken refuge with Octomasades, the above overtures effected a peace. The Scythian king

surrendered up his uncle, and received the person of his brother. Sitalces immediately withdrew his army, taking with him his brother; but on that very day Octomasades deprived Scyles of his head. Thus tenacious are the Scythians of their national customs, and such is the fate of those who endeavour to introduce foreign ceremonies amongst them.

81. On the populousness of Scythia I am not able to speak with decision. They have been represented to me by some as a numerous people, whilst others have informed me that of real Scythians there are but few. I shall relate, however, what has fallen within my own observation. Betwixt the Borysthenes and the Hypanis there is a place called Exampæus. To this I have before made some allusion when speaking of a fountain which it contained, whose waters were so exceedingly bitter as to render the Hypanis, into which it flows, perfectly unpalatable. In this place is a vessel of brass, six times larger than that which is to be seen in the entrance of Pontus, consecrated there by Pausanias, the son of Cleombrotus. For the benefit of those who may not have seen it, I shall here describe it. This vessel, which is in Scythia, is of the thickness of six digits, and capable of containing six hundred amphoræ. The natives say that it was made of the points of arrows, for that Ariantas, one of their kings, being desirous to

ascertain the number of the Scythians, commanded each of his subjects, on pain of death, to bring him the point of an arrow. By these means, so prodigious a quantity were collected that this vessel was composed from them. It was left by the prince as a monument of the fact, and by him consecrated at Exampæus. This is what I have heard of the populousness of Scythia.

82. This country has nothing remarkable except its rivers, which are equally large and numerous. If, besides these and its vast and extensive plains, it possesses any thing worthy of admiration, it is an impression which they show of the foot of Hercules. This is upon a rock, two cubits in size, but resembling the footstep of a man. It is near the river Tyras.

Washing, Cleansing, Scouring Everything.

A Pure Dry Soap, Fine Powder.

Hudson's Extract of Soap

From Cottage to Palace, Ships, &c.

In Packets One Penny and upwards

"MONTSERRAT" LIME-FRUIT JUICE.

From THE LIVERPOOL JOURNAL OF COMMERCE, *February* 20, 1886.

"The *Hilda* has just reached the Mersey from Montserrat her entire cargo, consisting of 50,000 gallons of lime-juice being the first arrival of the new crop. The demand for this article is increasing to such an extent that it may be of interest to the public to know that 180,000 gallons were sold during twelve months by the sole consignees, Messrs. EVANS, SONS & Co., Wholesale Chemists, Hanover Street, Liverpool."

In reference to above, the public would do well to see that "Montserrat" Lime-Fruit Juice and Cordials only are supplied, and that the Trade Mark is on the capsule as well as label of each bottle.

Sold by Druggists, Grocers, Wine Merchants, &c EVERYWHERE.

THE RIGHT HON. W. E. GLADSTONE *recently remarked*: "This reminds me of an admirable passage in a book which I hope will always be 'a HOUSEHOLD BOOK in England—I mean 'GULLIVER'S TRAVELS,' by DEAN SWIFT."

CASSELL'S ILLUSTRATED QUARTO EDITION OF
Gulliver's Travels

By DEAN SWIFT. With Explanatory Notes and a Life of the Author by J. F. WALLER, LL.D., and Eighty-eight Illustrations by the late T. MORTEN. **5s.**

"Mr. Morten's illustrations throughout are excellent, capitally drawn, and most humorous. . . . The explanatory notes, showing the political allusions in the tales, are necessary to the right understanding of Swift's object in writing them; they are ample and to the purpose."—*Art Journal*.

"We never so thoroughly enjoyed the plain, unvarnished tale so truthfully and plainly told by Captain Lemuel Gulliver, as the perusal of it in these pages. Never before did we so completely master the difference of the size between the traveller and the Lilliputians, and between the same and the Brobdingnagians; while the voyage to Laputa, which was only readable by a determined man, now becomes a labour of absolute pleasure. All this difference is owing to the pictures, which are strewn broadcast throughout the volume."—*The Bookseller*.

Popular Novels by Manville Fenn.
In Cloth, 2s. each.

THE VICAR'S PEOPLE.	**MY PATIENTS.**
SWEET MACE.	**THE PARSON O' DUMFORD.**
DUTCH THE DIVER.	**COBWEB'S FATHER.**
POVERTY CORNER.	

"Mr. Manville Fenn is one of the rare novelists who practise a delicate profession conscientiously. His successive books show unmistakable progress."—*The Times*.

Cassell & Company, Limited, Ludgate Hill, London; and all Booksellers.

Popular Novels by W. Westall.

The Old Factory. CHEAP EDITION, cloth, **2s.**

Red Ryvington. CHEAP EDITION, cloth, **2s.**

Ralph Norbreck's Trust. CHEAP EDITION, **2s.**

"There is invention and spirit and 'go' in Mr. Westall's novels, as well as an invariably healthy tone and a sufficiently close adherence to the ways and habits of man as actually observed, to justify them from the charge of unreality."—*Manchester Guardian*.

Cassell & Company, Limited, Ludgate Hill, London; and all Booksellers.

> "May children of our children say,
> 'She wrought her people lasting good;
> Her court was pure; her life serene;
> God gave her peace; her land reposed;
> A thousand claims to reverence closed
> In her as Mother, Wife, and Queen.'"
>
> TENNYSON.

In Monthly Parts, *price* 7d.

The Life and Times of Queen Victoria.

With Illustrations on nearly every page

Part 1 ready MAY 25, 1886, price 7d.

*** *With* **Part 1** *will be issued, free of charge, a* **Large Presentation Plate** (*size* 25 *in.* × 20 *in.*), *consisting of Handsome Engraving of the Picture by* GOURLAY STEEL R.S.A., *entitled* "A Cottage Bedside at Osborne."

"The Life and Times of Queen Victoria" will show how profoundly the momentous events of the past half century have been affected by the character and influence of Her Majesty. The work will contain a multitude of anecdotes illustrating the personal life of the Queen, and exhibiting those traits which have so thoroughly endeared the Sovereign to her people. The **Engravings**, moreover, will be full of interest as they will represent all the memorable scenes in the life of Her Majesty, with portraits of the various eminent men and women of the time.

*** *Prospectuses may be obtained of all Booksellers, or post free from*

CASSELL & COMPANY, LIMITED, *Ludgate Hill, London.*

Now Publishing, *Monthly*, **1s.**

EGYPT: DESCRIPTIVE, HISTORICAL, AND PICTURESQUE. By Prof. EBERS.

With about **800 ORIGINAL ILLUSTRATIONS.**

"Of all the numerous works on Egypt that have come from the press, none can compare with Professor EBERS' splendid description."—*Record.*

"The text presents as useful an account of the country and its innumerable marvels as can be desired by the ordinary reader, and the illustrations, which appear on nearly every page, are furnished by a combination of artists whose names are a guarantee of excellence."—*Times.*

"'EGYPT: DESCRIPTIVE, HISTORICAL, AND PICTURESQUE,' is as entertaining as it is valuable. The illustrations are singularly attractive; they include examples of almost every subject which can serve to bring the history, the arts, and the people of Egypt vividly before the eye of the reader."—*Spectator.*

Cassell & Company, Limited, Ludgate Hill, London; and all Booksellers.

Just Published, *price* **1s.**

OUR COLONIES AND INDIA: HOW WE GOT THEM, AND WHY WE KEEP THEM. By CYRIL RANSOME, M.A. OXON.,

Professor of Modern Literature and History in the Yorkshire College, Leeds.

"An excellent little handbook of the question that has just appeared by Prof. RANSOME. This little book, which is published by Messrs. CASSELL, contains a plain, unvarnished statement of the steps by which we gained our colonies, and of the reasons, sentimental and commercial, why we keep them."—*The Times.*

Cassell & Company, Limited, Ludgate Hill, London; and all Booksellers.

READY SHORTLY, *price* **1s.**

Great Northern Railway Official Illustrated Guid[e]

ILLUSTRATED THROUGHOUT.

Almost every page in this popular Guide will [be] studded with high-class Engravings of places of n[ote] on the Great Northern Railway. A complete ser[ies] of Route Maps, illustrating the several sections [of] the line, has been specially executed, together wi[th] "Bird's-eye View" Maps, printed in colours, whi[ch] show the entire extent of the Great Northern Syste[m] indicating the whole of the country on either side [of] the line.

N.B.—The following OFFICIAL ILLUSTRATED GUID[ES] have been reprinted to meet the large and continuous dema[nd] for them:—

- The Midland Railway Official Illustrated Guide, 1s. or cloth, 2s.
- The Great Western Railway Official Illustrate[d] Guide, 1s.; or cloth, 2s.
- The London and North Western Railway Offici[al] Illustrated Guide, 1s.; or cloth, 2s.

Cassell's Illustrated Guide to Paris, 1s.; o[r] cloth, 2s.

Cassell & Company, Limited, Ludgate Hill, London; and all Booksellers

---

A CLASSIFIED CATALOGUE

giving particulars of upwards of ONE THOUSAND VOLUME[S] published by CASSELL & COMPANY, ranging in price from **Threepence to Twenty-five Guineas,** will be sent on request *post free to any address.*

Cassell & Company, Limited, Ludgate Hill, London.

FIVE GOLD MEDALS
BORWICK'S
BAKING POWDER
FOR CAKES, PASTRY & PUDDINGS.

The Best in the World. THE LARGEST SALE IN THE WORLD

To Make a G[ood] Plain Cake.—Mix together one pound of [flour;] two full teaspoonfuls [of] BORWICK'S GOLD ME[DAL] BAKING POWDER, a [pinch of] salt and spice, and a [quarter] of sugar; rub in a ¼ [lb of] butter, add six ounce[s of] sultanas, two ounces of [cur]rants, and one ounce of [can]died peel; moisten the w[hole] with two eggs, and h[alf a] teacupful of milk previ[ously] beaten together; bake [in a] quick oven very thorou[ghly.]

Sold by all Grocers, Stores, Corn Dealers, Oilmen, &[c.]

PRACTICAL GUIDES TO THE STUDY OF
Water-Colour, Oil, and China Paintin[g]

Animal Painting in Water Colours. With [16] Coloured Plates by FREDERICK TAYLER, late President of the R[oyal] Society of Painters in Water Colours. Crown 4to, cloth. **5s.**

China Painting. By FLORENCE LEWIS, of the Lamb[eth] School of Art. With 16 Coloured Plates. **5s.**

Water-Colour Painting, A Course of. *Eighth* [and] *Enlarged Edition.* With 24 Coloured Plates from Designs [by] R. P. LEITCH. **5s.**

Tree Painting in Water Colours. With 18 Colou[red] Plates by W. H. J. BOOT. **5s.**

Flower Painting in Water Colours. *First* [and] *Second Series.* With 20 Coloured Plates by F. E. HULME, F.[L.S.,] F.S.A., in each. **5s.** each.

Painting in Neutral Tint, A Course of. With [24] Plates by R. P. LEITCH. **5s.**

Figure Painting in Water Colours. With 16 Colou[red] Plates from Original Designs by BLANCHE MACARTHUR and JE[NNIE] MOORE. **7s. 6d.**

Sepia Painting, A Course of. With 24 Plates f[rom] Designs by R. P. LEITCH. **5s.**

Sketching from Nature in Water Colours. [By] AARON PENLEY. With Illustrations in Chromo-Lithography [from] Original Water-Colour Drawings. **15s.**

Landscape Painting in Oils, A Course of Lesso[ns] in. By A. F. GRACE, Turner Medallist, Royal Academy. With [Many] Reproductions in Colour. *Cheap Edition.* **25s.**

Cassell & Company, Limited, Ludgate Hill, London; and all Booksel[lers.]

www.ingramcontent.com/pod-product-compliance
Lightning Source LLC
Chambersburg PA
CBHW020930230426
43666CB00008B/1621